Sto ...a m... ...vide the said triangular ... two straight angle triangles, each of which is kept respectively at right angles to each side of the oblong net aforesaid by means of loops and strings, and is fixed to pegs driven in the ground.

The large oblong net forms the dividing wall of the court, and the triangular net the wings or side walls thereof, whilst the floor is marked out by paint, coloured cord, or tape into "in" and "out" courts, serving as crease, right and left courts, and boundaries. By this simple apparatus a portable court is obtained by means of which the old game of tennis, which has always been an indoor amusement, and which few can enjoy on account of the great expense of building a brick court, may be made an outdoor one, and placed within the reach of all, as the above described portable court can be erected in a few minutes on a lawn, on ice, or in any suitable sized space either in or out of doors.

SPECIFICATION in pursuance of the conditions of the Letters Patent, filed by the said Walter Clopton Wingfield in the Great Seal Patent Office on the 22nd August 1874.

TO ALL TO WHOM THESE PRESENTS SHALL COME, I, WALTER CLOPTON WINGFIELD, of Belgrave Road, Pimlico, in the County of Middlesex, send greeting.

WHEREAS Her most Excellent Majesty Queen Victoria, by Her Letters Patent, bearing date the Twenty-third day of February, in the year of our Lord One thousand eight hundred and seventy-four, in the thirty-seventh year of Her reign, did, for Herself, Her heirs and successors, give and grant unto me, the said Walter Clopton Wingfield, Her special licence that I, the said Walter Clopton Wingfield, my executors, administrators, and assigns, or such others as I, the said Walter Clopton Wingfield, my executors, administrators, and assigns, should at any time agree with, and no others, from time to time and at all times thereafter during the term therein expressed, should and lawfully might make, use, exercise, and vend, within the United Kingdom of Great Britain and Ireland, the Channel Islands, and Isle of Man, an Invention for "A NEW AND IMPROVED PORTABLE COURT FOR PLAYING THE ANCIENT GAME OF TENNIS," upon the condition (amongst others) that I, the said Walter Clopton Wingfield, my executors or administrators, by an instrument in writing under my, or their, or one of their hands and seals, should particularly describe and ascertain the nature of the said Invention, and in what manner the same was to be performed, and cause the same to be filed in the Great Seal Patent Office within six calendar months next and immediately after the date of the said Letters Patent.

(Continued on back endpaper)

Stroke Production
in the Game of Tennis

By the same authors:

THE GAME OF SINGLES IN TENNIS
THE GAME OF DOUBLES IN TENNIS

Stroke Production
in the Game
of Tennis

by

William F. Talbert and Bruce S. Old

Drawings by Katharine D. Old

J. B. LIPPINCOTT COMPANY

Philadelphia and New York

The drawings on pages 24, 74–77, and 78, by Ed Vebell, originally appeared in *Sports Illustrated* magazine and in *Sports Illustrated Book of Tennis*, J. B. Lippincott Company, Philadelphia and New York; copyright © 1958, 1959, 1960, by Time Inc.

The drawing on page 98 was adapted by Katharine D. Old from a photograph courtesy of *World Tennis* magazine, and originally appeared in *The Game of Singles in Tennis* by William F. Talbert and Bruce S. Old, published by J. B. Lippincott Company, 1962.

Foreword

Any tennis player, young or old, girl or boy, beginner or expert, can profit immensely from reading and studying this superbly illustrated presentation of the fundamentals of the game. Every important aspect of stroke production is covered, as well as ways of motivating players, equipment selection, footwork, how to practice, a bit on tactics and, for the first time in any sport, a photographic exposition on the art of anticipation. In a lightning-fast sport such as tennis, the ability to anticipate is a prerequisite to progress toward local, national and international greatness.

I have always been impressed with the soundness of the teachings of Bill Talbert, many times a champion and also a U. S. Davis Cup Captain. He has contributed greatly toward making the game of tennis a sport for everyone. Working in partnership with him is Bruce Old, and this team has produced the two most popular and basic books ever written on tennis tactics, *The Game of Singles in Tennis* and *The Game of Doubles in Tennis*. I cannot commend to you too highly this new book by these authoritative authors. Together the three volumes represent a complete set of the best teachings in tennis.

PANCHO GONZALES

Contents

CHAPTER   PAGE

Foreword   5

1. INTRODUCTION   9

2. WORKING WITH THE BEGINNER   19

3. THE SERVE   39

4. THE GROUND STROKES   65

5. NET PLAY   100

6. IMPROVING YOUR GAME   115

LIST OF ILLUSTRATIONS

End Papers. Letters Patent No. 685

Figure 1.	The Classic Eastern Forehand Drive by Ralston	12–15
Figure 2.	The Eastern Grips of William T. Tilden	23
Figure 3.	The Eastern Grips of J. Donald Budge	24
Figure 4.	The Continental Grip of Rodney Laver	25
Figure 5.	The Western Grip of William M. (Little Bill) Johnston	26
Figure 6.	Talbert's Short Backswing Serve	30
Figure 7.	The Concave Volley Wall	37
Figure 8.	The Three Basic Serves	41

Figure 9.   Gonzales's Serve   42–47
Figure 10. Ashe's Flat (Cannonball) Serve   48–56
Figure 11. Ashe's Slice Serve   57–58
Figure 12. Ashe's American Twist Serve   59–60
Figure 13. Ralston's Spin Serve   61–63
Figure 14. Kramer's Forehand   67–69
Figure 15. Tilden's Forehand   70
Figure 16. Graebner's Forehand   71–73
Figure 17. Budge's Backhand   74–77
Figure 18. Baseball Analogy   78
Figure 19. Rosewall's Backhand   79–81
Figure 20. A Low Ralston Backhand   82–84
Figure 21. Topped Cross Court Passing Shot by Mrs. King   85–87
Figure 22. Ashe's Dink Shot   88–89
Figure 23. Gonzales's Lob   91
Figure 24. Selecting a Receiving Position   92–93
Figure 25. Backhand Down the Line by Mrs. King   94–95
Figure 26. Forehand Down the Line by Mrs. King   96–97
Figure 27. Gonzales's Chip Return of Service   98
Figure 28. Mrs. King's Standard Forehand Volley   101–03
Figure 29. Ralston's Backhand Volley
              —with Something Taken Off   104–06
Figure 30. Mrs. King's Stop Volley   107–08
Figure 31. Ashe's Swinging Volley   109–11
Figure 32. Mrs. King's Overhead   112–14
Figure 33. Aim Points for Return of Service   118–19
Figure 34. Anticipation Sequence by Mrs. King   126–30

Table.   Major Tennis Court Differences   136

CHAPTER 1

Introduction

The objective of this book is to provide a simple, yet authoritative, basic text on the fundamentals of the great game of tennis. It is aimed at coaches and teachers as well as players. We have attempted to make it useful for all classes of players, from beginners to tournament circuit regulars, irrespective of age. In short, we hope the book will be of assistance to any player or coach trying to improve his skill and to enhance the enjoyment he obtains both from playing and from instructing others.

This book should be read slowly and reread from time to time. It is difficult to absorb the material all at once, and it is easy to forget some of the important fine points and fall into bad habits. Although we do not wish to frighten the reader, tennis is not a simple sport. It requires practice, speed, stamina, courage and generalship. As the great champion William T. Tilden described it, "Tennis puts an athlete under the hardest physical, mental and nervous strain of any game played by mankind." But it is also true, and comforting to know, that almost anywhere in the world you can invariably find a tennis enthusiast of your own caliber to play with as you develop your skill and enjoyment of this universally popular sport.

The modern game of tennis grew out of the ancient Greek game of σφαιριστικὴ, the Roman game of "Pila" and the fashionable court tennis game played in the palaces of the kings of France and England beginning in the fourteenth and fifteenth centuries.

It remained for an Englishman, Major Walter Clopton Wingfield, to popularize the sport by inventing the game of lawn tennis. For this he was awarded Letters Patent No. 685 (see end papers) on July 29, 1874. Since the Major's game of tennis requires only relatively inexpensive grounds and equipment, yet provides excellent exercise for the participants and excitement for the spectators, the sport spread within a few years to all corners of the earth. As evidence of the soundness of the game, it has gone through few rule changes in the intervening years.

Although there are no accurate figures available on the number of people who play tennis the world over, the total probably exceeds 20 million, making tennis just about the most popular participant sport. Obviously such an international sport must be properly governed, and it is highly desirable that all tennis players understand how this is accomplished.

As is the case with all recognized international amateur sports, there exists for tennis an international sports governing body. This body, organized in 1913, is called the International Lawn Tennis Federation. The Federation has a combined active and associate membership of some eighty-nine nations. Its purposes and objectives are, broadly, to provide unity and action, to establish, uphold and publish the rules and rule changes in various languages, to promote teaching, to promote participation, to promote the international lawn tennis championship (Davis Cup) and to sanction all international tennis events.

In order for citizens of any nation to compete in international events, a nation must have its own national tennis association and that association must be a recognized member of the International Lawn Tennis Federation. For example, in the United States the national sports governing body, formed in 1881, is called the United States Lawn Tennis Association.[1] It is responsible for encouraging participation in tennis, establishing rules of play and eligibility for United States citizens, fostering sportsmanship and fair play, holding national championships, sanctioning open and international tournaments and developing the sport. By developing, we mean that the sports governing body must provide leadership in broadening the base of participants, particularly youngsters; in seeing that facilities such as outdoor and indoor courts are provided; in encouraging coaches and instructors to furnish sound, basic teaching by providing instructional films and sponsoring coaching clinics under the supervision of experts; in undertaking special training and conditioning of particularly talented youngsters; and in promoting international seasoning of players by sending teams abroad and inviting foreigners to participate in this country.

[1] Address: 51 East 42nd Street, New York, New York.

Naturally, all of this requires that the sports governing body maintain both a sound administration and a strong financial position. Therefore, it is important that each reader consider becoming a dues-paying member of his sports governing body and taking an active part in its operations. In this way he may participate effectively both as a contributor to the development of tennis as a sport and as a player eligible to compete in officially sanctioned tournaments.

No one book can cover all the intricacies of tennis. The authors have covered tactics in two previous books on singles and doubles.[2] Therefore, this book will concentrate almost entirely on the methods of preparing for and producing the basic strokes. To make the many instructive suggestions as easy to understand as possible, we will resort to extensive use of drawings. All the drawings were made from high-speed movies of experts. We selected for depiction only strokes that result in successfully executed shots.

There are a number of general factors that are important to recognize before we consider the art of stroke production.

Background of the Basic Points

Three things characterize all great tennis players. First, they make the game look relatively easy because they all utilize proper and early stroke preparation methods. These entail sound footwork and fluid, simple, seemingly effortless motions with perfect balance and timing, resulting in economy of motion and energy. Second, they all produce the various strokes within fairly narrow limits of orthodox style concepts at the moment of hitting the ball, although each player maintains a certain individuality matched to his physical makeup and prowess. No two players have exactly the same stroking form. In other words, even though there are certain basic stroking principles, there is no single perfect method of hitting a particular tennis stroke. And third, they have practiced and played so much that they anticipate the opponent's strokes and court position and invariably make the proper answering shot despite the fact that the time to think about the shot is usually limited to fractions of a second.

2 *The Game of Doubles in Tennis* (Philadelphia: J. B. Lippincott Company, 1956). *The Game of Singles in Tennis* (Philadelphia: J. B. Lippincott Company, 1962).

Figure 1.

The Classic Eastern Forehand Drive by Ralston

a

Frame a. Here we see Dennis Ralston in excellent ready or anticipatory position. The racket is pointed toward the net, knees are bent slightly and weight is on the balls of the feet as he studies intensely the opponent's shot and anticipates the direction and speed of the approaching ball. At this instant he is just beginning to move to his right as he sees the ball coming to his forehand side.

Frame b. Ralston has started his run to the right by pivoting his right foot and pushing off with his left to bring it forward and across. In perfect balance, he is already starting his backswing high in a looping motion which, after the ball is struck and the stroke is finally completed, will almost trace a figure eight laid on its side (∞). His left hand is still on the racket, which forces Ralston to turn his shoulders to the right in the proper manner.

Frame c. The move to pivot the body to the right continues here with beautiful balance as the knees are bent and the weight more

b

c

on the ball of the right foot.

The shoulders are turning to the right as the racket backswing is at the high point of the figure eight, and the left hand is being brought forward for balance. It is important to recognize that this smooth preparation is made well before the ball has arrived. Many beginners tend to wait too long and are forced to make the backswing hurriedly in a jerking motion when the ball is already on top of them.

Frame d. At this point the racket is lowered and starting forward as the shoulders begin turning to the left and Ralston's weight is shifting forward toward the left foot.

d

e

Frame e. For the first time the ball is now in sight, and the racket head is down near the bottom part of the loop, moving forward in perfect coordination with the forward weight shift of the body. Note that the shoulders are now parallel to the net, and they continue to turn to unleash the force of the drive. Very importantly, the knees are bent to allow Ralston to get well down to the ball. This permits him to watch the ball as it meets the racket and to hold the racket more firmly, as well as to maintain better balance.

Frame f. The left arm is extended for balance. The stance is closed (lead foot nearer the right sideline than the back foot), which indicates he will hit the ball down the line or to his right rather than cross court.

At the moment of impact the weight is still shifting forward, the knees well bent, the ball struck properly just in front of the left foot to direct it straight down the line as the racket starts up and over with face a bit open to apply top spin and sidespin. To direct the ball cross court, it would have to be hit a bit earlier with more open stance (lead foot nearer the left sideline than the back foot) and top spin (see Figure 16d, page 72). The shoulders are pivoting, and the forearm, wrist and racket are now locked in a straight line to put power into the shot. Note that Ralston has his eyes glued to the ball.

The trajectory of the ball was such that it cleared the net by the safe margin of about 2 feet and landed near the opponent's base line. The experts seldom play against the odds by hitting net-skimming spectaculars. Only when their opponent is at net in the volleying position do they aim closer to the top of the net.

14

f

Frame g. The follow-through is beginning here with the racket coming up, face somewhat open, to slide the ball down the line as the shoulders and hips continue to turn toward the net. Body balance is smoothly maintained and shifted totally onto the left foot to add body momentum to the force of the stroke.

Ralston's footwork in this sequence is excellent. Without footwork to move into the proper court position while maintaining balance, you cannot strike the ball with regularity and power. It is said that Ellsworth Vines worked all of 1929 to 1930 on improving his footwork. He then dominated world tennis for the next several years.

Frame h. The follow-through is now complete, the racket high over the left shoulder. The weight is being distributed to both feet as Ralston prepares to return to the ready position to await the answering shot. Only with such solid stroke completion can the full power of the stroke be realized. The entire stroke is so rhythmical that it appears effortless.

g

h

We will attempt to present as clearly as possible the stroke production methods utilized by the expert players as well as the methods recommended for beginners. Although it might appear to be puzzling that there should be any difference between the two methods, some differences are indeed necessary during the learning process, depending in part upon the age, strength and athletic capabilities of the particular beginner. Certainly you cannot expect to begin with the stroking form, timing and power of an expert in tennis any more than you can expect beginners to hit a pitched baseball the way Ty Cobb, Joe DiMaggio, Ted Williams or Willie Mays could, or a stationary golf ball the way Bobby Jones, Ben Hogan, Arnold Palmer, Gary Player or Jack Nicklaus does. Achieving good form is an evolutionary process.

Every tennis stroke contains certain fundamental motions similar to those used in many games or sports. Perhaps the most familiar is that of throwing a ball. The act of throwing for any distance requires continuous movements consisting of bringing the throwing arm back as the shoulders turn and the weight is shifted to the back foot, moving the arm and turning the shoulders forward swiftly as the ball is released and simultaneously shifting the weight ahead to the forward foot in the important follow-through motion. The free arm is used, in addition to the feet, for balance throughout the motions. Roughly similar movements of arms and shoulders and weight shift also occur when one is hitting a baseball, swinging a golf club, executing a long hook in boxing, casting with a fishing rod, batting in cricket, hitting a handball or throwing a discus in track.

In order to assist in orienting the reader, let us sneak in a brief preview of a classic, orthodox style applied to one of the most used strokes in tennis, the forehand. This example will help in understanding the terms we will be using throughout the balance of the book to describe various actions. In Figure 1 we see eight selected frames from a high-speed film showing Dennis Ralston hitting a standard eastern forehand drive in classic style.

Physical Conditioning

The late U. S. singles champion, Lieutenant Joseph Hunt, who also played varsity football for Navy, always classified tennis as the more grueling sport. It is essential that a player who wishes to advance within his or her bracket develop real stamina. In fact, in any long match, whether a local playground event or on the center court at Wimbledon, the player in better physical condition can, and often has, defeated the man who is supposedly a better player.

More will be said on this subject in Chapter 6.

Spin on the Ball

The flight of any ball is controlled by spin, and the tennis ball is no exception. The reader may be more familiar with this phenomenon in other sports. The famous knuckle ball used by some baseball pitchers is thrown without spin. It moves so erratically that most big-league catchers have adopted the practice of using extra-large gloves in order to have a chance of just stopping, let alone catching the ball. In football a forward pass must be thrown with a spiral motion or else the ball will wobble wildly and seldom reach its intended receiver. Similarly, all accurate guns are bored with spiral rifling in order to give the projectile the necessary spin to keep it on course, free from tumbling and yawing. And a golf ball is also kept on line by its numerous small dimples which give it stabilizing spin and lift. Without these dimples, a smooth golf ball has a violently erratic and inaccurate flight. We will talk more about the importance of spin on the tennis ball in Chapter 3.

CHAPTER 2

Working with the Beginner

Interesting the Youngster

Children vary in their development, coordination and interest in sports. Most youngsters are not able to hold and wield a tennis racket until they are about nine or ten years old. Thus the youngest age-group tournaments recognized by most lawn tennis associations is for twelve-year-old and under girls and boys. However, there are examples of children from four to eight years with natural aptitudes who pick up the game and play. So the proper age to begin depends on the particular youngster and his interests.

It is often best to start a youngster by working with him in performing simple exercises that will develop his coordination. For example, there are a number of games of fun that just involve throwing a tennis ball. Elementary games of catch teach a young hopeful the importance of keeping his eye on the ball. Introducing variations, such as catching on the bounce, allow him to learn to judge how a tennis ball behaves. Throwing the ball to his right, left, short or over his head so that he has to run to catch the ball on the first bounce teaches movement and footwork. If you add to this the requirement that the youngster throw the ball back as soon as possible after making the catch, you teach him balance at the completion of his run similar to that which he needs in playing tennis. Gradually learning to throw the ball back for distance will bring out the vital importance of the proper length of backswing, the shifting of the weight forward as the ball is released and the long follow-through. If no one is around with whom to play, the beginner can still practice by throwing a tennis ball against a wall or steps, preferably not too near a window. Trying to see how many successive balls he can catch without an error can make an exciting game even when he is all alone.

Getting the youngster to the tennis court the first few times is usually up to his parents or some of their tennis-playing friends. It is not possible to speculate on all the situations one might encounter, but probably the most important thing to try to avoid is boredom. The little fellow should not be left just to dig in the dirt or climb, but encouraged to swing a racket and hit some balls. Maybe he will have to grip the racket with two hands and swing it like a baseball bat, but let him get the thrill of banging some over the net that even his big father cannot return. Participation and fun are the goals of the hour, with the paramount objective being to keep the youngster wanting to come back for more. Pleading to stay on and on, or to return with his pals in tow, is the first sign of a budding tennis enthusiast.

The role of the parent in generating the interest of a sibling in tennis, as in any other sport, is a delicate one. Opinions vary all the way from forcing participation to ignoring sports altogether and letting the child decide. We tend to prefer a middle-of-the-road path, tailored to the character of the particular child. And, of course, children vary from A to Z in their reactions to parents. In talking with teaching professionals we note with great interest that they find that most young people between sixteen and twenty-five who do not play adequate tennis wish their parents had been more insistent in getting them to participate as youngsters. This is because they realize at this age that tennis is a great social sport and that it is easiest to learn at an early age. How then are the parents best able to urge gently without having their children revolt because of a feeling of domination? The greatest asset working for the parents is the genuine respect, however well hidden, most children have for them. This vital asset the parents should continue to exploit by the intelligent and sensitive application of positive leadership. It is usually wise to lead with a silk thread, not a hawser. So much for our child psychology lesson—if you have a problem, it might be better for you to consult someone who is actually qualified!

Having taken a pass at presenting a careful, diplomatic approach to encouraging a child to play tennis, let us try to develop a deeper understanding of the real importance of sports participation to child and adult alike. We have studied the literature from several nations on this subject. At the outset it is important to note that any statements on human behavior must be general in that while they may apply to a majority of cases, exceptions are always to be found. Research to produce substantive data on the value of athletics is always clouded by the complexity of human beings and the difficulty of obtaining controlled samples of the population. Nevertheless, our research has led us to the following assertions, which we believe to be sufficiently reliable to deserve careful study by both adults and children:

The health benefits of wholesome exercise are now well substantiated, and are just as pertinent to the female as to the male.

There are indications that the healthy youth who participates in athletics also performs better in his studies. Participation in competitive games can lead to the development of qualities that are useful to society as well as to the individual—by sparking the motivation or drive for success, by teaching youth a system of formal rules governed by a concept of "fair play," and by instilling the code of "sportsmanship" which, though difficult to define in the abstract, is a trait which people around the world understand and respect.

Some of the more successful efforts by church and welfare organizations to combat juvenile delinquency in urban areas have involved instituting active neighborhood athletic programs as a means of channeling the physical energy of children and youths into socially acceptable forms of play.

Participation in healthful physical recreation is now accepted, and rightfully, as contributing to the feminine image instead of detracting from it.

In brief, the evidence indicates that amateur sports can perform a useful role in developing the individual and strengthening the ethical fabric of society. Given the proper direction and support, sports can become a powerful force for enriching the variety of our experience, for alleviating some of the social problems of the underprivileged and for encouraging the pursuit of excellence in still another dimension of endeavor. Finally, sports at the international level can play an important role in bringing about understanding and friendship among the peoples of the world.

All of this should give you the hope and assurance that the great day will come when your daughters and sons and pupils thank you sincerely for the many hours you have devoted to their development of sports appreciation.

Let us assume that we now have our girls and boys to the point of desiring to learn to play tennis and that they are about ten to twelve years old. In this age group few children have the size of hand to grip the racket or the physical strength to hit tennis strokes in a manner similar to the top adults. This weakness presents an extremely interesting problem. Actually, the teacher is faced with showing the child the *wrong* way to make certain strokes at this age in order to allow the pupil to hit the ball with sufficient force to achieve some skill and pleasure. For example, consider the serve. A child can best learn to stroke the ball by gripping the racket with the eastern forehand grip in order to combine a stiff wrist and forearm behind the racket. This enables him to have the power to hit the ball over the net into the service court. But as we shall see in more detail in Chapter 3, this is the wrong service grip for the adult player who has the strength to obtain speed and spin by whipping the racket through the ball with his wrist. The same sort of compromise in technique is necessary in the production of some other strokes.

Thus proper teaching of the youngster requires that the instructor be very sensitive to the capabilities as well as the motivations of his pupil. Timing is an important part of the entire picture. While it is necessary in the early stages to teach in a manner that makes it easiest for the child to hit the ball and have some fun rallying, it is also essential to understand when he is ready to be weaned from the game of the beginner to the more advanced methods of the adult.

Before we go into the subject of teaching the beginner, some words of explanation and caution are required. First, we should point out that the detailed information on the recommended techniques of producing each of the major strokes is presented in later chapters. Therefore, rather than duplicate such details in this chapter, we will cover only the more salient features as they may apply to the beginner. Second, as a result of this first point of limitation, it is important that the reader recognize the necessity of studying the remaining portions of this book in order to understand more completely this particular section. Perhaps the easiest thing to do when you do not understand a point is to turn to the illustrations in the later chapters for clarification.

Gripping the Racket

One of the first steps is to learn the ways to hold a racket and the names given to these grips, because we refer to them often in the book.

Currently there are two basic racket grips, the eastern and the continental. We have selected the grips of Tilden, Budge and Laver as illustrations for the pupil. Any objections to that choice? For good measure we include the western grip of Johnston. These grips are shown in Figures 2, 3, 4 and 5.

Note that Tilden did not put his thumb up the back of the handle on his backhand, as does Budge. Ken Rosewall, the owner of one of the greatest of all backhands, does not either, since he believes there is seldom time to do so. Also, because of lack of time to make grip changes, the continental grip is the standard grip for all top net players.

Figure 2.

The Eastern Grips of William T. Tilden

a

Tilden demonstrates (a) his classic eastern forehand grip with the palm of the hand and wrist directly behind the racket face to allow the application of maximum power.

b

The eastern backhand (b) is obtained by rotating the racket about a quarter turn to get more hand and wrist behind the shot.

The standard service grip (c) is a slightly modified eastern backhand grip.

c

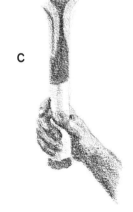

Figure 3.

The Eastern Grips of J. Donald Budge

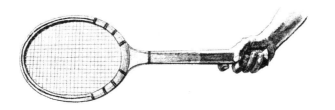

a

Budge's eastern forehand grip (a) is very similar to Tilden's. It is often described as shaking hands with the racket.

Note that the racket handle extends slightly behind the heel of the hand.

The eastern backhand and service grip (b) has the hand on top of the racket with the V between thumb and forefinger pointing to the left shoulder. For his ground strokes Budge extended his thumb back of the handle as shown.

b

Figure 4.

The Continental Grip of Rodney Laver

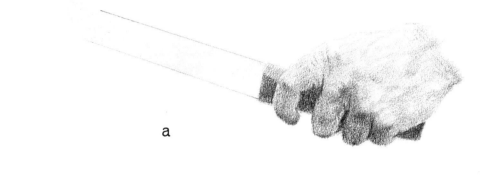

a

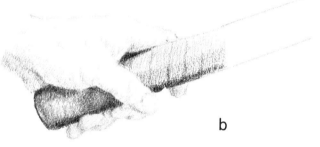

b

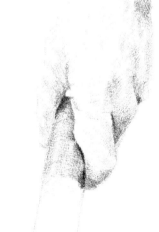

c

These three drawings show views of left-handed Laver's continental grip which he uses for all strokes from the forehand (a), backhand (b) and top (c) sides. The grip is essentially midway between the eastern forehand and backhand grips.

This grip demands a strong wrist and is usually not recommended for beginners. The continental grip is, however, recommended for all net play. Its particular advantage is that you can hit volleys from either sides or overhead without changing your grip, and you seldom have time to change grips in rapid-fire net play.

Figure 5.

The Western Grip of
William M. (Little Bill) Johnston

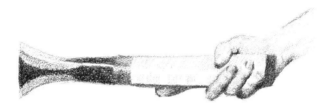

The western grip used so effectively by Johnston and others in the 1920's is seldom seen today. As shown, the hand is a quarter turn more to the right than in the eastern forehand to provide top spin to the shot. Johnston used the same grip for the backhand by turning his wrist over and hitting the ball with the same side of the racket as in the forehand.

Working with the Young Beginner

The selection of a racket depends on the size of the pupil. There are specially made, small, inexpensive rackets for the very young beginner. For most, a standard (27 inches long, 9 inches wide) racket weighing 12 to 12½ ounces is recommended. The grip should be the smallest standard size, which is 4⅜ inches.

The first lessons should deal with the forehand as that is the easiest stroke for most people to learn. One good method is to place the child just back of the service court line, standing sideways to the net and facing toward the sideline. This is close enough to the net so that he can hit the ball over it without too much effort. At the outset it is well to teach the rhythm of the swing without a racket. A simulated swing—just bringing the arm well back until it points toward the base line, swinging through the hitting area as the weight is shifted forward and following through so shoulders turn and the arm is pointing toward the net—will give the pupil a feel for the motions of the stroke.

The next step is to let the pupil hit a ball. You should place the racket so that his hand and wrist are behind it as in the eastern forehand grip. If the racket is too heavy, place his hand part way up the handle (in the "choke" position) so that it is better balanced. First let him practice the swing just as he did without the racket. When he gets the rhythm of the complete motion, get ready to drop the ball. With the pupil's forward foot just behind the service line, drop the ball about 3 to 4 inches in front of the line and far enough from the body so that the natural, level, waist-high swing of the racket will meet the bounding ball squarely in the center of the strings. At first let him start with his racket back at the end of the backswing, with feet apart and weight balanced, so that the motion is merely that of swinging forward and through the ball.

Once the young hopeful is hitting them over the net with some regularity and is grinning with the pride of accomplishment, the sequence can be made increasingly difficult, as well as more fun. This entails moving in stages toward the ready position with the pupil facing the net and going through all the motions of turning, setting the feet and making the entire stroke.

The ready position is essentially the same for all strokes. We prefer to call it the anticipatory position to continually remind the player that in this position he must try to anticipate the direction and speed of the opponent's shot as the first step in readying himself to make the return. We will have more to say later in Chapter 6 about how to anticipate. (Any time the reader is curious, he may want to peek at this important sequence of drawings.) The anticipatory position is the position not only for the start of each stroke but also for the finish, since you must return to the position as rapidly as possible in order to be on the alert for the opponent's next shot. The anticipatory position is shown by Dennis Ralston and Mrs. Billie Jean King in Figures 1a and 28a. The racket is held loosely, normally with the eastern forehand grip (unless at the net, where the continental grip is usually recommended). The left hand cradles the racket gently near the throat and helps to point it toward the net with the head slightly upward. Elbows are close to the sides. The body is relaxed and bent forward from the waist to place the weight on the balls of the feet, and the knees are bent a little. The feet are set at about the width of the shoulders, and the toes are pointed out somewhat as this permits you to push off and get a more rapid start to the right or left. With the racket pointed toward the net you are in position to turn with equal speed to intercept returns to your forehand or backhand. Small variations in the anticipatory position are used in the return of service which will be reviewed later.

Now to return to our beginner. Place him in the anticipatory position about 18 inches back of the service court line and have him go through the motions of the complete forehand stroke. This entails pivoting on the right foot and bringing the left foot across and forward while bringing the right arm back and turning the body and shoulders sideways to the net. At the same time the weight shifts first to the right foot and then to the left as the player steps forward into the shot with the left hand out for purposes of balance. This sequence of motions should be practiced for a time without benefit of a ball until the beginner learns the natural rhythm of the stroke. Once this is mastered, you can time the drop of a ball just ahead of the service line so that as he pivots and swings the racket the bouncing ball will be at proper height for the stroke. After a few tries he will be whacking the ball over the net with gusto.

The next step is to toss the ball toward him until he learns to judge the bounce and move to the ball, position himself properly, get his racket back in time and produce the stroke. Then you can cross to the other side of the net and hit balls at the young hopeful until he gets the knack of producing his first realistic tennis strokes. The racket should travel in the classic figure eight demonstrated by Ralston in Figure 1b (page 13).

Now that the pupil is hitting a moving ball it is necessary to impress upon him how important it is that he watch the ball all the way in to the racket. Somehow you have to communicate the message that the experts believe that four out of every five errors in tennis are due to inattention. "Keep your eye on the ball!" is a phrase that must be indelibly printed on the mind of beginner and expert alike.

The same sort of routine should next be carried out with the backhand stroke. The grip should be the eastern backhand grip and the shoulder turn emphasized (see Figure 3b, page 24) so that the pupil can employ his strength to best advantage to execute the stroke. A helpful hint in this connection is to teach the pupil the importance of the free hand with which he is cradling the racket while in the anticipatory position. If he maintains that hand gently on the racket as he performs his backswing, it is impossible for him not to get the full shoulder turn so important to hitting the ball with pace (see Figure 17, pages 74–77). For the right-hander, the motion is much like swinging a baseball bat left-handed (see Figure 18, page 78).

The most difficult stroke to teach the beginner is the serve, since it requires several coordinated motions. (If the child is too young, he can begin by serving with an underhand forehand.) You should start the beginner by working on the toss. Use only one ball, held loosely between the thumb and first two fingers. It is important to teach release of the ball near the top of the movement of the left arm. This movement starts with the elbow close to the body and the arm out at hip level pointing to the net, and continues upward until the arm is straight overhead (see Figure 9a, page 43). By such a sequence you can best insure that the toss is accurate as to height and direction and that the timing and rhythm of the entire service stroke begins in the proper manner. The second major motion is with the right arm. It can be described as being similar to throwing a ball overhand or to standing up and driving in a nail with a powerful stroke of a hammer at the top of your reach. The next trick is to get the two motions going together and in sequence with proper timing. The shortened backswing, demonstrated by Talbert in Figure 6, is perhaps the easiest for the beginner to adopt.

The whole motion should be practiced first with just a ball and no racket. As soon as the pupil gets the rhythm down, try the stroke with a racket and no ball. The racket should be held with the eastern forehand grip to gain strength in the swing. Finally, place the beginner at the service court line with left foot toeing the line and right foot about 12 inches back and start him trying to hit the serve into the service court opposite. The left foot should remain stationary and the right foot should come forward as the weight shifts when the ball is struck. This will not come easily, so the teacher has to be patient. But once a ball lands successfully in the court, joy will prevail. The pupil is then on his way as a tennis player, and soon he will be able to play from the base line just like all the older youngsters whom he admires.

Once our beginner has learned the basic ground strokes and serve, it is best to try to get him to play enough to master these to the point where he can have fun playing with his friends before you teach him lobs, volleys and so on. Some dedicated youngsters will practice alone against a wall or backboard by the hour, but most want to be with the rest of the gang and do whatever they are doing. The first problem is getting the beginner over a certain

Figure 6.

Talbert's Short Backswing

Frames a, b, c, d. Talbert demonstrates the similarity of motion between throwing a ball and the backswing of the serve (a and b). The toss essentially complete, Talbert's weight is shifting forward as he is bringing his racket up to stroke the ball (c). Talbert has just hit the ball with racket properly extended to full height (d). His right foot has come forward to put his weight behind the shot, and he is directing his attention to the position of his opponent as he is about to follow the serve in to net.

30

b

c

d

threshold level of play, so that he can beat one or two of his friends and develop some interest in the game. Next, it is the aim of every instructor to attract a mob of both girls and boys to the courts and to make this *the* place to meet and have fun. Group lessons and group practice are practicable. Age-group ladder competition for rankings and mixed round-robin tournaments run properly can generate all kinds of enthusiasm. Often it helps if the competition is so popular it is necessary to qualify in order to play. Important hints by the instructor during such events should include stress on rhythmic, fluid strokes, watching the ball while hitting and keeping the ball in play rather than slugging it spectacularly into the net or backstop.

Youngsters learn rapidly by their ability to imitate others, so it is well to expose them to good play by taking them to see tournaments. And if possible to arrange, a chance to rally even a short time with an outstanding player can provide a world of inspiration. Almost all great stars can recall some such event which stimulated their climb upward and are always ready and willing to help youngsters.

All the patient teaching, parental time and interest and hours of practice on the part of the pupil will ultimately be repaid many times over in satisfaction to all through the joy of years of healthy exercise and social pleasure gained by our young beginner from a whole lifetime of tennis activity.

Working with the Older Beginner

The older teen-ager or adult beginner represents a different type of teaching assignment. This is not just because of the added physical strength and ability to understand a more sophisticated explanation of the finer points of stroke production techniques, but also because of a desire for privately oriented rather than group lessons. This natural feeling is brought about by a desire to acquire some ability to hit the ball before being subjected to the critical stares of friends and acquaintances.

Rackets for the adult vary between 13 and 15 ounces in weight, with grip sizes from $4\frac{1}{4}$ to $5\frac{1}{4}$ inches. Also the rackets balance at various points near the midpoint of their 27-inch length, so that they are head or handle heavy, or balanced. Trying out various combinations is required to find the particular racket which best matches your hand size and stroke techniques. As one grows older the tendency is to go toward a lighter racket, whether wood or metal frame.

Once again it is best to start with the forehand. But this time you can place the subject on the base line and first demonstrate for him the grip and the details of the swing, with emphasis on the shoulder turn, the backswing, the weight shift as you swing through the ball and the follow-through necessary to finish the stroke. Let the pupil swing through with knees slightly flexed a few times to get the feel of the rhythm of stroke. Once you are satisfied with the form of the pupil, get his feet set just back of the base line, body sideways to the net, and drop the ball on a line 3 or 4 inches ahead of his left foot so he can have his racket arm properly extended and weight behind the shot as he swings through to meet the ball. The pupil should be sure to keep his eye steadily on the ball throughout the stroke and aim to hit the ball about 3 feet above the net in order to give proper depth to the shot as well as to avoid netting the ball.

An important thing to demonstrate is the need to finish the stroke with a complete follow-through. One of the advantages of the eastern forehand is that it fails miserably as a stroke unless it is completed. It is easy to show that stopping the follow-through causes the ball to sail in uncontrollable fashion, whereas swinging the racket through the figure eight properly to end at shoulder height (see Figure 1h, page 15) imparts a slight top spin to the ball which keeps it within the playing surface. In fact, once the student gets the feel of his wrist firmly behind the racket on a solidly hit ball, the whole stroke sequence will fall readily into place, since it is basically a natural motion.

The backhand is a less natural motion, and many adult beginners, in particular the girls, tend to get a complex about it and run around the ball to get it on the forehand if at all possible. Actually, however, once learned it is almost as easy a stroke as the forehand. The basic trouble most girls have is that they fail to get ready for the ball in time and thus end up at the last second trying to push the ball, with awkward, disastrous results. The key to overcoming this problem is to begin the body turn and the backswing as soon as the ball starts over the net toward you, keep the left hand on the racket near the throat to guide it back and help force the full shoulder and body turn, get the weight mostly on the left foot and learn to transfer the weight through to the forward foot as the ball is struck (see Figure 17, pages 74–77). Fortunately this motion is easy to practice without a ball until it becomes automatic. Then it can be practiced with a ball dropped a few inches in front of the right foot to get the timing right, before undertaking to position yourself properly for a ball being hit to you. The older beginner has the ability to practice to advantage by himself against a backboard in order to iron out in relative seclusion any feeling of awkwardness.

The serving motion is also liable to make the adult feel like an uncoordinated fool at first. The toss of the ball should be the easiest thing to practice and learn to do in adequate fashion, with arm extended straight up at the finish of the toss. The thing that has to be worked on is the timing of the backswing and weight shift to develop a coordinated swing. Just going through the motions, at first without a ball, will help to make the pupil feel at home. And, once again, the eastern forehand grip and short Talbert backswing make the knack of the motion less complicated to acquire. When the rhythm of the motion is obtained and a ball is used to practice the stroke, it is very important to make the pupil keep his eye on the tossed ball as he strikes it, because a common error is to look too soon toward the direction of the serve. If the server can develop the habit of always looking intently at the tossed ball, he will normally acquire a good striking motion.

Once the beginner learns this simple, reliable serve, it is easy to build upon the basic elements to develop more advanced services. As a first step, it will in most cases be desirable, particularly for the men, to change the service grip to the eastern backhand grip. Since this is explained fully in Chapter 3 on the service, it is only necessary to say at this point that the eastern backhand grip is preferred because it permits better utilization of wrist action.

Because the older beginner is usually asked to play social doubles by his friends more often than is the youngster, it is also important for him to learn to volley at the outset. Volleying is not only an important element of doubles; it is also lots of fun and relatively easy to learn. The key points to remember are:

1. Keep the body sideways to the net at the moment of volleying, with knees bent so the ball is struck with the head of the racket above the grip (see Figure 7, page 37). For some reason girls hate to bend their knees, so the fairer sex will have to work particularly hard on this necessary factor. Getting down to the ball like this is essential, for it allows you to follow better the flight of the ball into the racket and to grip your racket with necessary firmness.

34

2. Using a short backswing and a short follow-through, hit the ball with a stiff wrist and a punching motion about 6 inches in front of the forward foot. This motion, coupled with step 1 above, will permit you to watch the flight of the ball all the way into the racket (see Figure 7, page 37). 1589846

3. Since the volley must be struck quickly while the ball is still in flight, it is necessary to be ready to hit from either the forehand or the backhand side. For this reason the better players use the continental grip (Figure 4, page 25), which is equally effective for forehand or backhand and thus avoids any time loss in changing grips. Also, it is necessary to hold the racket pointing toward the net when in the anticipatory or ready position, with the left hand cradling the racket near the throat, in order to help you turn with equal rapidity to either side.

The best way to understand the entire sequence of the volley is to think of the firm wrist and racket as presenting a solid wall inches in front of your body, against which the ball strikes and rebounds over the net into the opponent's court. Another way of thinking about the action is that it is like catching a ball a few inches in front of the body, with the racket face substituting for your hand. To simplify things let's ignore sharp-angled and stop volleys, since these require special touch and tactical openings, and concentrate on the standard net player's goal of a deep volley to keep the opponent on the defensive.

The proper volleying technique is both important and, fortunately, easy to learn. We can advantageously begin at the vertical midpoint of the volley stroke with a waist-high volley. As shown in Figure 7, Dennis Ralston strokes the waist-high volley, eyes glued on the ball meeting the racket and wrist below the racket head, positioning the racket face essentially perpendicular to the ground about 12 inches in front of his body. For a ball at this height the racket position is correct, as you do not have to direct the flight of the ball up or down in order to hit an effective deep volley. By way of contrast, Billie Jean King, in hitting a low volley in Figure 28d, page 102) has her racket face well open, or laid back, in order to propel the ball upward over the net and also deep into the opponent's court.

Now let us look at the simulated racket angles and positions for volleys as they vary with height of volley (Figure 7). In a very real way we find that there is indeed presented, as previously mentioned, a firmly locked wrist and racket wall against which the ball will impact. Thus the low volleys are hit with the racket face open to hit the ball up over the net, and the high volleys are directed deep and downward with a closed racket face. As shown, the low and high volleys are hit slightly forward of the waist-high volleys so that the wall the volleyer presents to the passing shot is slightly curved or concave, as indicated by the dotted line. For the high volleys the body and racket arm should be moving forward at impact to provide pace.

It is very helpful for any tennis player, whether beginner or veteran, to understand the principles of the volley concave wall. Whenever the volleyer tends to make errors or short volleys, he should reconsider the fundamentals of the eyes on the ball and a stiff wrist with the hand below the racket head.

Practicing volleys is great fun. The best procedure is to position a player on each side of the net just in front of the point where the three service court lines come together, which is known as the T. The players, or instructor and player, should then try to volley the ball back and forth. The reason for standing so far back from the net is that each player gets more opportunities to hit low volleys, which are the most difficult to make. You are forced to learn to bend those knees, keep your wrist below the racket head and get ready rapidly to receive the return, or it will pass you. At doubles tournaments you can watch the great doubles players practice this way and keep the ball flying back and forth for minutes. Once you get the knack, it is great sport. Then when you move into the regular volleying position, 6 to 9 feet from the net, you will find that drives hit at you from the base line will be much easier to volley.

To impress upon you the importance of bending the knees in order to keep the racket head above the wrist, we would like to get technical for a moment. The muscles in the human arm are constructed in such a way as to allow you to grip an object hardest when the wrist is in the middle position. This is the position in which the fist is clenched in line with the forearm which is in the normal middle position, pictured by Ralston in Figure 7. If Ralston were to reach for a low ball by dropping the racket head straight down by the sole motion of breaking or extending his wrist, he would lose gripping power. (See a similar motion by Arthur Ashe in Figure 22d where he extends his wrist on purpose to achieve backspin.) We tested both male and female tennis players for grip strength, using

36

Figure 7.

The Concave Volley Wall

a grip-power measuring device. In each case the players lost close to 20 percent of their middle-wrist gripping strength when extending the wrist into a downward position. (Wrestlers have long used the technique of bending an opponent's wrist to break his grip.) When you couple this loss in grip strength with the loss in ability to follow the ball into the racket because you are standing up straight and far away from the flight path of the ball, you can encounter serious trouble. In effect, you compound the sins of poor stroke production technique. You are less likely to be able to hit the ball in the center of the racket when the eye is farther from the line of flight of the ball; at the same time you are less able to grip the racket firmly to offset an off-center impact of ball on racket. An error is very likely to result. This is a lesson that all tennis players must learn if they are to climb into the class of the accomplished player. Fortunately, it should be easy to master once it is understood.

So much for our beginners, young and old. It is now time to see how the experts hit the ball, because imitating the best of their techniques will lead to the sound tennis strokes upon which enjoyment of the game, competency and greatness can be built.

CHAPTER 3

The Serve

In the modern forcing game employed by top singles and doubles players the serve is probably the most important stroke in tennis. This is because it sets the stage for subsequent action at the beginning of each point. Before we get into stroke production techniques it is important that the reader understand a number of basic principles.

There are major differences between proper serve and volley tactics for singles and those for doubles.

In singles, depending on the speed of the court surface, the serve can (1) win the point outright through an ace or by drawing an error (which occurs 18 to 30 percent of the time), (2) force a weak return which can be hit away for a winner (which occurs 5 to 15 percent of the time), (3) permit an outright loser from a devastating return of service (which occurs 12 to 15 percent of the time) or (4) result in the normal return which brings about an exchange of shots to determine the ultimate winner of the point (which occurs 40 to 60 percent of the time).

In singles the decision to follow the serve in to net centers around the ability of the serve to draw a defensive return. This depends in large measure on the speed of the court surface, since the serve is about twice as effective on a fast grass court as on a slow clay court. Those small differences in speed of bounce provide the alert receiver with invaluable potential advantages.

In doubles the approved tactics call for the server to follow every serve in to net because of the outstanding advantage enjoyed by the team occupying the net position. The doubles serve is less potent as an outright winner (about 18 percent of the time) than the singles serve because most players slow the first serve down a bit in order to get it in more frequently. But a good first serve and first volley

39

combination wins about 40 percent of points in doubles, whereas the outcome of the rest of the points is dependent on an exchange of shots. The second serve is a different story. It is only half as effective as a first serve and spells joy to the receiving team, as it can move in to hit the ball down at the feet of the advancing server and work on engineering a service break.

To become a truly effective server you have to learn to accomplish three difficult assignments. First, you must strive to get your first serve in, setting a goal of about 80 percent of the time. The importance of this is clearly evident from the fact that first serves ultimately win points, about 4 or 5 to 1 over second serves. Second serves are normally slower and thus permit the receiver to move forward 3 or more feet and make the return with more confidence and authority from a better attacking position. Second, you must hit both serves deep so that they land within 3 feet of the service line. To serve shallow is to give away the advantage of the serve, since the server will ultimately win only about half of the short-serve points. And third, you have to be able to keep the receiver guessing by moving him around with different service spins and placements.

The first step toward acquiring a good serve is to adopt the most appropriate service grip. Most good players use the eastern backhand, as this particular grip provides the wrist freedom to permit you to hit the flat, slice or twist serve with little change in motion. These variations keep the opponent off balance. Players vary from using a closed-finger baseball grip to using one in which the fingers are spread on the racket as is typical for backhand ground strokes. The grip is kept light until just before impact with the ball in order to allow the wrist to remain supple and bend to provide maximum wrist snap as the ball is struck. This snap imparts both speed and spin to the ball.

There are three classes of serves used in tennis today. We will show the motions for each as demonstrated by various experts.

The difference between the flat, slice and American twist serves (the old reverse twist is seldom seen) is in the spin imparted to the ball. This can best be explained by picturing the tennis ball as a clock. The flat serve is hit by directing the racket straight at the clock to the center where the two hands are attached. The slice serve is hit by bringing the racket around, down and across the face of the ball and striking it at about the 3 o'clock position to provide a right-to-left spin. The toss for this serve should be slightly more to

Figure 8.

The Three Basic Serves

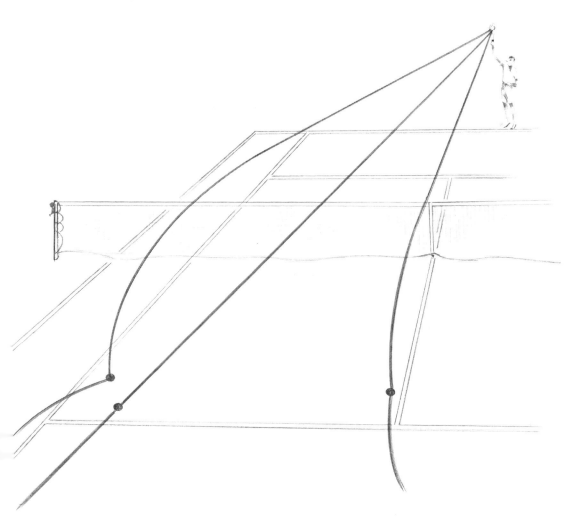

William Talbert demonstrates the trajectories and bounces of the three basic serves. From left to right these are the American twist, flat and slice serves.

41

the right. The American twist serve requires a toss more to the left, almost directly overhead. The ball should be struck up and over at the 10 to 11 o'clock point with a snapping wrist action. This puts a wicked spin on the ball, allowing you to hit it high over the net to avoid serving errors. On landing, the ball takes a high kick to the left toward the opponent's backhand. The American twist is a standard first serve for doubles and second serve for singles. The three types of serves are schematically demonstrated by Talbert in Figure 8, page 41. The various serving motions will be clarified by studying the subsequent drawings of the styles of the experts.

Gonzales's Serve

Certainly Richard A. (Pancho) Gonzales owned the greatest serve of the long, exciting era from about 1948 to 1962, during which he dominated first amateur, and later professional, tennis. Not only did he have a serve measured at a speed around 110 miles per hour, but he also hit the ball with uncanny accuracy. We actually counted his serves in a match on grass at Forest Hills when he was at his peak and found he put 86 percent of his first serves into play. That is one of the major reasons he was so hard to beat—his good, deep first serve usually resulted in an ultimately victorious point three out of four times. The Gonzales serving motion is so smooth the ball seems deceptively soft until it jars the racket in your hand. There is a lesson here, as struggling to add power often introduces jerky motions that actually reduce the severity of the shot.

Figure 9.

Gonzales's Serve

Frame a. First note the position of the feet for the serve. Gonzales, standing near the center of the base line, places his left foot just behind the line at an angle of about 45 degrees. The right foot is about 12 to 15 inches back and a little to the right of the left foot to facilitate its later forward movement.

The Gonzales toss is classic, with the left arm fully extended, the racket arm fluid and relaxed, the shoulders turned perpendicular to the net, the knees slightly bent and the weight slightly on the left foot. The grip is a compressed eastern backhand variety approaching the baseball grip. The straight, extended left arm toss is essential for accuracy and height of toss, without which a cramped or badly timed serve will result.

The toss itself should be just high enough to reach the hitting zone, which is where the racket center is when your arm is extended fully overhead. You want to hit the ball at that precise moment between its rise and fall when it is not moving. If you toss the ball too high, it will be descending rapidly, thus presenting an additional timing problem. If you toss too low with a crooked left arm, you lose some of the service court target areas and are prone to net the ball. Develop a rhythmic serve and avoid "chasing" the ball with quick motions. The toss should be about an arm's length in front of you so that you can hit the ball as your body is moving forward in order to get maximum weight and power into the stroke.

Practice of the toss may seem dull, but believe us when we say it will pay off more than you will ever hope. Jack Kramer attributes the excellence of his serve to the accuracy of his toss.

a

Frame b. This is a beautiful picture of the coiled Pancho ready to unleash a bomb. The back is arched, the racket (though you cannot see it) is dropped so it is pointing straight down with wrist cocked, the eyes are focused on the ball, the weight is on the toes and the left hand is out for balance.

b

Frame c. Gonzales has whipped the racket up as his wrist is uncocking and his arm extending. His weight is moving forward on the ball of his left foot, eyes on the ball and left arm down to get out of the way of the hit as well as to help the weight shift. The shoulders are turning, with left shoulder down, and the right foot is moving forward.

d

Frame d. Just after impact the racket arm is fully extended, the wrist is locked behind the racket squared for a flat serve, the shoulders are turned so that the right shoulder now leads, the right foot is crossing the base line and the left leg is straight to add height to the impact point.

46

Frame e. The complete follow-through really gives the best indication of how hard Gonzales has hit his serve. You can almost feel the impact of all 185 or so pounds of unleashed fury as Pancho finishes his powerful shoulder and hip turn and brings his right foot forward to begin his run to the net to volley the return (if any!).

Gonzales always put a slight spin even on his "flat" serve in order to gain control. After he turned professional he shortened his service backswing somewhat to gain accuracy and conserve energy.

e

Ashe's Services

Arthur Ashe, despite the fact that he does not possess a rugged, muscular build, has one of the fastest serves of the current tennis greats through the exercise of great body and wrist action and timing. Especially in 1968, when he won the first Open Singles Championship at Forest Hills, his serve was devastating. That same year we were fortunate to take a number of high-speed movies of him as he demonstrated for us the three basic serves.

Figure 10.

Ashe's Flat (Cannonball) Serve

a

Frame a. Ashe is standing in perfect position, with left foot 45 degrees to the base line and feet about 12 to 15 inches apart, as he starts the racket down and begins his toss with the left hand. His weight is slightly on his right foot.

Figure 10, pages 48–56, shows the complete service action, including the six-step run to the net and the first volley.

It should be evident from the descriptions of the different types of service by Ashe that the toss is a vital part of the stroke. To repeat, it requires a lot of practice to be able to get the toss high and in the proper position. Inaccurate tosses are responsible for most serving errors. Failure to watch the ball at the moment of impact causes many of the other errors.

b

Frame b. The racket is now at the bottom of the swing back as the tossing arm continues upward. The weight is starting to shift forward, and the left knee is bent slightly.

Frame c. The ball has been released as the left arm is now straight and the racket head is waist high. The left knee is bending more while the weight shifts almost entirely to that side.

Frame d. As the racket arm continues upward and the wrist starts to cock, the weight is now essentially all on the ball of the left foot as the right foot is brought forward with the toe on the ground. Both knees are bent. The shoulders are turned perpendicular to the net.

50

e

Frame e. The racket arm is now approaching the completion of the backswing. At the completion Ashe's elbow will be pointed upward, the racket straight down and the back slightly arched, as in the slice and American twist serves shown in Figures 11 (pages 57–58) and 12 (pages 59–60). His body is now leaning well into the court, the knees are straightening to push off and gain height and all the weight is on the left foot. The left hand has come down to clear the hitting zone and help maintain balance.

f

Frame f. Ashe has just completed contact with the ball and has broken his wrist straight downward on the flight path of the ball, as is characteristic of the flat serve. His legs, body and racket arm are in an extended straight line in the same fashion employed by Tilden and other great servers. The shoulders have turned straight toward the net to add power. The left hand is brought in to help balance against the forward motion of the racket arm. Note particularly the feet. The current foot-fault rule allows both feet to leave the ground as long as neither one touches inside the base line prior to striking the ball. Ashe has taken every advantage of this rule by pushing with his left foot as the right foot comes over the line so that his right foot is almost a step into the court when the ball is struck. This gains him an important split second in his run to the net position.

Frame g. Ashe's right foot has not quite touched the ground as his run to the net begins. The follow-through after the snap of the wrist is continuing, and the racket face is almost flat with respect to the receiver in the forehand court. The racket arm is fully extended, and the left hand is tucked in to the chest to help the balance.

Frame h. Ashe is completing his second step in the court as he races with body still bent forward from the tremendous follow-through of his flat service stroke. His eyes are on his opponent to try to anticipate the type of return.

53

Frame i. At the third step in the court Ashe has taken a more up-right position and is bringing his racket forward toward the ready position.

Frame j. In this particular sequence Ashe did not employ the technique used by most serve and volley artists which entails bringing both feet together by taking a half step with the right foot after four long strides to attain the anticipatory position. This frame shows Ashe in the characteristic hopping position, also used in the return of service, from which he can move rapidly to the left or the right to intercept the return.

Since the return of service in the sequence that we photographed was obviously going cross court, Ashe elected not to take the hopping position here depicted, but continued his run, swerving to his right, as shown in Frame k.

54

Frame k. During his fourth step toward the net Ashe has noted that the return of service will be a good, low shot cross court to his forehand and is, therefore, starting to shift his run slightly to his right with his racket in ready position.

Frame l. During his fifth step Ashe begins his backswing with racket high and shoulder turning back. His left hand is extended for balance, and his right knee is well bent as he starts to get down low to half volley a good, low service return. Note that the service line has come into view.

55

Frame m. At a point just inside the T of the service courts Ashe is completing his sixth step, watching intently the approaching ball.

Frame n. The ball has just bounced in front of Ashe's racket, and he is completing a half volley, with the face of the racket properly nearly perpendicular to the ground to keep the return low. Ashe has gotten well down to the ball by bending his knees so that his wrist is near the level of the racket head. This is the classic method of making the half volley with a sidearm rather than underspin motion.

56

Figure 11.

Ashe's Slice Serve

Frame a. The backswing is standard as the elbow points up and the racket head is straight down at the completion. The back is slightly arched.

Frame b. As the racket head moves up it is pointing almost straight back while Ashe turns his body and shoulders toward the net. This form coupled with the toss of the ball a bit to the right and about 10 inches in front of the head is the tell-tale signal of the slice service for which the alert receiver must watch.

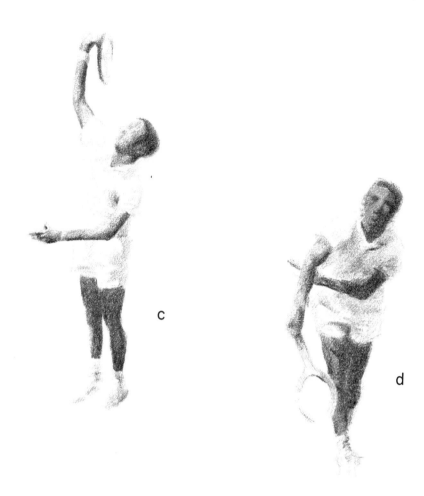

c

d

Frame c. At close to the moment of impact you can see from the position of the racket that Ashe is about to slice (hit around, down, and over the ball at the 3 o'clock position mentioned on page 40). Note that he is almost facing the net and is hitting the ball over his right shoulder.

Frame d. At the finish Ashe's racket is still in the slice position in front of his right leg. This ball landed in the forehand corner of his opponent's service court, and the strong spin caused it to curve about 5 feet off the court beyond the sideline after the bounce.

58

Figure 12.

Ashe's American Twist Serve

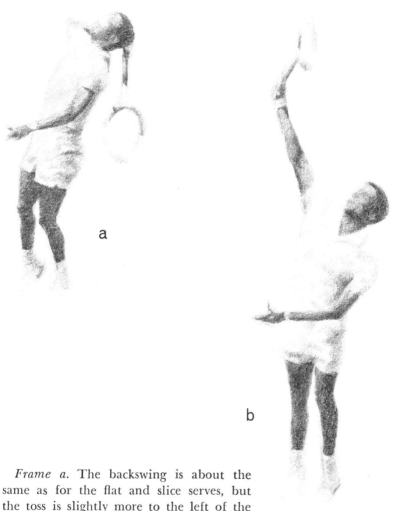

a

b

Frame a. The backswing is about the same as for the flat and slice serves, but the toss is slightly more to the left of the head and the back is more arched.

Frame b. As the racket comes up before impact Ashe is facing more to the right sideline and has his back slightly arched (see the Ralston sequence in Figure 13, pages 61–63, for closer detail).

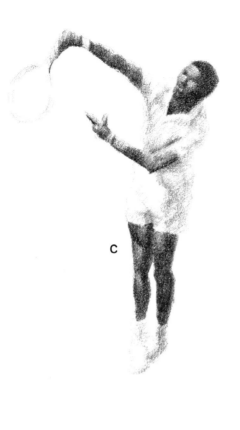

c

d

Frame c. Ashe has just struck the ball at the 10 to 11 o'clock position by snapping his wrist, whipping his racket up and over the ball and following through to his right toward the sideline. The shoulders are still facing to the right in contrast to the slice serving action. This action imparts a terrific spin which carries the ball high and safely over the net (about 3 feet), lands it deep in the receiver's court and causes a high reverse bound to the backhand of the opponent.

Frame d. The finish of the follow-through is to the right of that of the flat and slice serves. Many top servers, for example, Jack Kramer, finish with the racket behind the advancing right leg to be sure the full twist spin is applied.

60

Ralston's Spin Serve

Dennis Ralston hits what he calls a spin serve instead of the true American twist. However, the close-up in Figure 13 shows the similarity of the great back and wrist action of this shot to that of the American twist serve.

Figure 13.

Ralston's Spin Serve

Frame a. Ralston has an exaggerated arch of the back at the completion of his backswing in order to be able to meet the ball tossed almost directly over his head.

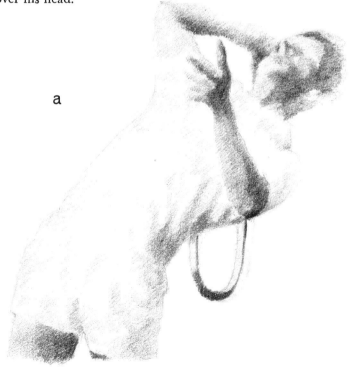

a

b

Frame b. As the racket arm comes up, the back starts to straighten to put force behind the racket head.

C

Frame c. The terrific force of the whipping wrist action is shown here as Ralston propels the racket head through toward the sideline. His shoulders are turned more toward the net than are Ashe's in the American twist serve.

63

CHAPTER 4

The Ground Strokes

The ground strokes have always been the backbone of the games of the great tennis players of history. However, for the past twenty-five years the highly developed serve and volley "big" game has dominated tennis singles, largely because the major championships have been played on fast grass courts. Currently there is a trend toward the use of slower artificial grass, composition and asphalt courts to reinstate the long, exciting rallies of the golden era of Tilden, Johnston, Lacoste, Vines, Perry and Budge. Thus, to the delight of the spectators, the ground strokes are regaining their exalted position as the framework around which a sound tennis game is built. Not surprisingly, the highly talented modern players, such as Gonzales, Laver and Rosewall continue to excel with the switch in surfaces.

To determine the importance of the surface on tactics, we made a comparison of winning strokes from singles matches played by the same top professionals on different courts. On grass, ground strokes produced 35 percent of winners, whereas on slower clay they accounted for half of all winners. Even a Gonzales cannot afford to follow service in to net consistently against a good receiver on a slow court, and the effectiveness of his other forcing shots and volleys is blunted.

In doubles it is essential to take the net position on each serve because of the overwhelming advantage of the attacking position. This reduces the ground stroke winners in championship doubles to about 25 percent of all winners (in club doubles the figure is closer to 40 percent). However, the ground strokes in championship doubles do represent about 40 percent of all strokes hit, so the need for developing sound execution cannot be downgraded. They provide the key to the all-important service break by forcing the weak volley or by maneuvering the net team out of position.

To develop dependable ground strokes takes hours of practice because of the concentration, timing and coordination needed to move and stroke properly a speeding, sometimes erratically bounding, tennis ball. A recommended method of practice is presented in Chapter 6. The experts like to take the ball on the rise from the bounce. This not only adds pace to the return but hurries the opponent.

In this chapter we attempt to illustrate a wide variety of ground strokes, executed by different players, in order to provide a sound basis for instruction. The reader should note particularly the beautiful rhythm that persists throughout all the strokes—beginning with proper footwork and balance, continuing with full use of body turn for power and ending with proper racket utilization to impart spin and direction to the ball and follow-through for pace and length.

The Forehand Drive

We will begin with the forehand drive, since this is the workhorse of most tennis players, whether weekenders or serious tournament competitors. It is the favorite weapon to move the opponent about, to force a weak return, to approach the net or to pass the volleyer.

Kramer's Forehand

One of the great forehand drives of all time was that of Jack Kramer, erstwhile amateur and professional champion. Kramer used the standard eastern forehand (see Figure 14).

Tilden's Forehand

We have slipped in here a drawing (Figure 15) of the forehand action of the most famous of all tennis players, William T. (Big Bill) Tilden. His form is perfect as he prepares to hit a forehand down the line, indicated by his left foot pointing toward the sideline and his right foot trailing in a closed stance. His shoulders are just turning toward the net from the perpendicular position as his weight shifts forward, his left arm extended for balance and his knees well bent. His racket-arm elbow is bent, and his wrist is solidly behind the racket in classic eastern forehand style. His eyes are glued on the ball (which is in line with his left hip).

Figure 14.

Kramer's Forehand

Frame a. Kramer starts to his right, having just released his left hand from the racket, shoulders turned, racket head high and elbow close to the body.

Frame b. The form here is perfect as Kramer, having reached back in the standard figure-eight pattern, now lowers the racket head near the level of the ball and prepares to bring it forward. His elbow remains bent, but his laid-back wrist and forearm are coming into line to provide the steely stiffness of the hitting section. The weight is on his back foot, and the left arm is out for balance.

67

c

Frame c. Kramer is about to strike the ball at the preferred position between knee and waist height. Although his stance is open, for two telltale reasons you should be able to anticipate that he will hit the ball down the line. First, he has waited to hit the ball late, nearer his right foot, contrasted to the early hit necessary for the cross court drive (see Clark Graebner in Figure 16, pages 71–73). And second, the racket head is still slightly back of the wrist to indicate again the down-the-line direction of the shot. The racket head is now below the ball in classic eastern style. The shoulders and hips are turning forward to put power into the shot. Eyes are concentrated on the ball. The stance in this case is open in contrast to Dennis Ralston's closed stance, with left foot closer to the sidelines, shown in Figure 1, pages 12–15.

Frame d. Kramer has just finished hitting the ball, his wrist slightly laid back to guide it down the line with sidespin and slight underspin. His weight has shifted to his left foot as his shoulders turn to face the net to provide power.

Frame e. The finish of the stroke is classic, with weight on the left foot and complete follow-through with racket high. Note the straight line from elbow to wrist to racket head. The racket face is turned over slightly to indicate some degree of top spin.

d

e

69

Figure 15.

Tilden's Forehand

We have slipped in here a drawing of the forehand action of the most famous of all tennis players, William T. (Big Bill) Tilden. His form here is perfect as he prepares to hit a forehand down the line, as indicated by his left foot pointing toward the sideline and his right foot trailing in a closed stance. His shoulders are just turning toward the net from the perpendicular position as his weight shifts forward, his left arm is extended for balance, and his knees are well bent. His racket arm elbow is bent and his wrist is solidly behind the racket in classic eastern forehand style. His eyes are glued on the ball (which is in line with his left hip). Note how closely this form compares with that of Kramer in Figure 14b (page 67) and Ralston in Figure 1c (page 13). Most great players exhibit the same form at the moment of impact.

Graebner's Forehand

In contrast to the nearly flat or slightly sidespin forehands demonstrated by Ralston (Figure 1f, page 15) and Kramer (Figure 14d, page 69), the stroke sequence exhibited by Clark Graebner in Figure 16 is a typical topped, cross court forehand drive.

Figure 16.

Graebner's Forehand

a

b

Frame a. Graebner shows good balance and concentration as he runs rapidly to his right to play a ground stroke hit down his forehand sideline. The racket head is high on the backswing, and the shoulders are turned perpendicular to the net in classic fashion.

Frame b. Here Graebner has reached the ball and planted his right foot to halt his run and prepare to stroke the ball. The racket head has dropped and will go below the ball in the familiar figure eight. The left hand is extended for balance.

d

c

72

e

Frame c. Graebner is just about to bring his racket up and over the ball to apply top spin. By his position you can tell he will hit the ball well in front of his left foot and direct the shot cross court. The shoulders are turning to impart force to the stroke.

Frame d. This figure shows clearly the application of top spin to the ball. The racket comes up sharply over the ball with a closed face. The forearm, wrist and racket are in one straight line. The momentum of Graebner's run for the ball continues to carry his left foot over and forward for balance. Note how well bent the knees are kept to permit him to get down to the ball to watch it all the way into the center of the racket and to maintain balance.

Frame e. The stroke is perfectly completed with racket face closed and high over the left shoulder for complete follow-through. The left foot is now planted, and Graebner is about to start moving rapidly to his left to get back into the ready position at the center of the base line.

The Backhand Drive

Many weekend players, particularly "les girls," have a phobia about the backhand and continually try to run around it to hit a forehand instead. Players who learn on slow courts, like clay, are especially prone to this disease. Some believe that the faster courts on which the Californians grow up have been responsible for forcing them to better develop a sound backhand early in life and that this has been a contributing factor to the string of great world-ranking players originating in that state.

Actually, the backhand is an easy stroke. It should be executed with the same mechanical principles as the forehand, constituting a series of simple, related steps performed in continuous motion. Properly struck, it is a dependable attacking weapon like the forehand. In fact, some people maintain it is easier to hit than a forehand because you are swinging away from your body with more freedom of motion.

To illustrate the stroke we have selected the two backhands generally recognized as the best in modern tennis history, those of Don Budge and Ken Rosewall, and have added those of Dennis Ralston and Billie Jean King for good measure.

Budge's Backhand

The backhand drive was the strongest stroke in Budge's repertoire. Figure 17 indicates why.

Figure 17.

Budge's Backhand

Frames a, b and c. Here Budge is turning from the ready position to meet the ball as it comes toward his left side. He takes a quarter turn of the grip to the left to get maximum wrist power behind his natural-motion, slightly imparted top-spin backhand. He moves so as to meet the bouncing ball below waist height.

a

74

b

c

d

Frame d. This frame is one that is worthy of careful study. It shows the completion of the backswing with the racket head high. Note that the left hand is still cradling the racket. Taking the racket back is a most important function of the left hand, since it forces the player to turn his shoulders and hips. Without the full body turn here exhibited by Budge, the striker cannot get power into the shot. The elbow is close to the body and pointing almost straight down, and the weight is on the rear foot.

Frame e. Here Budge starts to release his coiled energy. The arm begins to straighten, the racket head starts to drop just below the flight of the ball on the figure-eight path, the knees are bent as the weight shifts forward and the right shoulder is held down. The fingers tighten on the racket grip to prepare for impact.

Frame f. At the moment of impact the racket arm has straightened to meet the ball about 8 to 12 inches in front of the right foot and slightly below waist height at a comfortable distance so that the racket arm is neither cramped nor reaching, and the ball is hit dead center. The weight has shifted forward on the balls of the feet, and the shoulders and hips are turning to put all possible energy behind the stroke. The left hand provides balance. The eye is focused directly on the ball.

Frames g and h. The fluid, continuous, not jerky motion of the entire stroke is represented here by the smooth weight shift and complete follow-through as the shoulders and hips continue to turn and the racket head finishes high. The proper finishing of the shot to achieve full power is characteristic of the great tennis, golf, baseball and so on hitters. From the distance in front of the body at which the ball was hit and the direction in which Budge is looking on the follow-through, it is obvious he has hit a slightly cross court backhand.

Frame i. Here Budge is returning rapidly to the ready position to prepare for the expected return. No matter how well you have hit the shot, always assume your equally determined opponent will somehow get the ball back.

Figure 18.

Baseball Analogy

Budge demonstrates the similarity between the left-handed baseball swing of Ted Williams and Budge's backhand.

Rosewall's Backhand

Next to Budge's perhaps the greatest backhand in modern tennis belongs to Ken Rosewall, the diminutive Australian. One of the most interesting points is that he hits the ball quite differently from Budge, using an underspin rather than a slight top-spin shot. It proves that there is more than one way to produce an outstanding tennis stroke. Each player must adapt his own physical characteristics and natural feel for the game to the development of his stroke techniques. But as stated previously, the methods of all the great players have many points of basic similarity. Rosewall believes proper footwork is vital to a successful backhand. To reach greatness, Tilden took off a whole winter to work on his backhand footwork and stroke. The object is to get the ball just the right distance from the body for an uncramped, balanced swing.

Figure 19.

Rosewall's Backhand

Frame a. Rosewall has his weight a bit on his rear foot and his shoulders turned way back, elbow bent, racket high with face open and left hand still on the racket throat (although you cannot see it from this angle). The preparation for the stroke is much like that of Budge's in Figure 17d, page 75. Rosewall has shifted his grip about a quarter turn to the left, as does Budge; however, he does not put his thumb up the racket handle because this takes too much time in fast exchanges.

b

Frame b. The racket is being brought down to meet the ball with arm extending, weight shifting forward to the right foot, and left hand back for balance. Note how Rosewall has his eyes concentrated on the ball. He too will stroke the ball slightly below waist height.

Frame c. Rosewall has just met the ball only slightly in front of his right foot in order to guide it down the line. The racket face is slightly open to give the ball underspin. His weight continues to shift forward, knees bent and racket arm extended to a comfortable distance with wrist firmly locked. Note the similarity of form exhibited by Budge and Rosewall at the moment of impact. The only differences are that Rosewall's racket face is slightly laid back and he is hitting the ball farther back and closer to the body in order to direct it down the line. For the same reason his stance is more closed, with the left foot back.

Frame d. Rosewall is finishing the stroke with his racket face open and his weight all on his right foot. The fact that his shoulders and hips have turned only a little and that the follow-through is straight ahead clearly indicates he has hit the ball down the line rather than cross court. Contrast this finish with the cross court backhand being hit by Budge.

80

c

d

Figure 20.

A Low Ralston Backhand

In this series of drawings we see Dennis Ralston getting down beauti-
fully to a low, down-the-line backhand drive.

a   b

Frame a. The first position shown is at the moment that Ralston is
stepping in to a low bouncing ball to his backhand. His left hand,
having helped accomplish the full shoulder turn, is about to leave the
racket, and his right arm is beginning to straighten. As in the case of
Budge and Rosewall, his right shoulder is lowered to help meet the
ball. This classic form is essentially the same for all three players.

Frame b. Ralston is extending his arm with racket face open as he
bends waist and knees to get down to the trajectory of the ball to
better follow it into the center of his racket. The racket head has been
lowered into position to meet the ball as it comes into view. The weight
continues to shift forward.

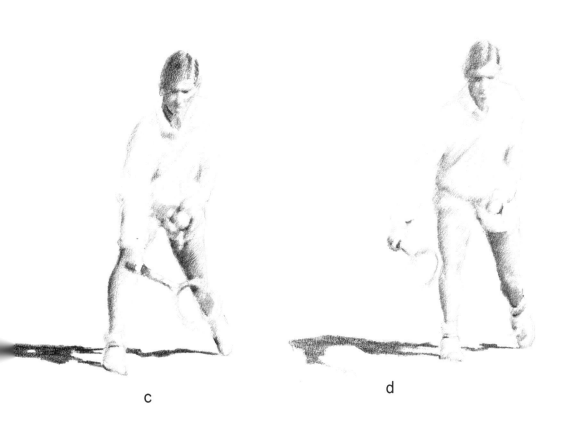

c

d

Frame c. At the moment of impact Ralston gets his weight into the shot by turning his shoulders and transmitting his forward movement to his right foot. He strikes the ball a few inches in front of his right foot with the face of his racket open and his locked wrist leading the racket head a bit to lend sidespin as well as underspin in order to direct the ball down the line. Note that the eyes are fixed steadily on the ball.

Frame d. Here the stiff wrist is still just leading the open racket, with great arm extension, to show the basic characteristics of the down-the-line backhand. All his weight is now properly on his right foot.

83

e

Frame e. Ralston has completed the follow-through in approved manner with arm extended and racket high above the shoulder. The fact that he hit the ball down the line is shown clearly. First, as in the Rosewall shot, his wrist has not rolled over and is still leading the racket. Second, in following the flight of the ball he is looking straight down the line.

84

Figure 21.

Topped Cross Court Passing Shot
by Mrs. King

This sequence shows Mrs. King hitting with gusto one of her favorite and best shots, a topped backhand cross court drive, to pass her opponent at net.

Frame a. The volleyer has made the mistake of hitting a volley that lands short, about 10 feet inside the base line. Mrs. King starts forward rapidly to meet the ball near the top of its bounce.

Frame b. Mrs. King has completed a normal backhand backswing with full shoulder turn as she stands just inside the base line.

85

c

d

Frame c. Now comes the first indication she will hit a top-spin shot as she drops the racket head almost straight down to allow her to hit up and over the ball which is just coming into view. Second, a cross court shot is indicated because she has brought her left foot forward and toward the sideline to open up her stance, and is preparing to hit the ball early. If the opposing volleyer were smart, she should start to move to the left the second this complete message is telegraphed.

Frame d. With her knees bent and weight shifted forward, Mrs. King swings her racket out, up and over the ball way out in front of her body (about 18 inches) in order to direct it cross court. Her eyes are concentrating on the ball, and her left hand starts out for balance.

86

Frame e. At the completion of the stroke she has put such force into the follow-through that she is up on her toes like a ballerina, with left hand fully extended for balance. The racket face is turned over, indicating the top spin.

Incidentally, the opposing volleyer was passed so quickly she hardly saw the ball.

The reader may wish to contrast this action with the down-the-line underspin backhand demonstrated by Rosewall.

e

The Dink Shot

The dink shot is hit essentially the same way from the forehand and backhand sides. Figure 22 shows Arthur Ashe producing a delicate dink approach shot against an opponent at net. To set the scene, Ashe has been given an opening in that his opponent's first volley bounces waist high some 8 feet inside the base line. Noticing that his opponent is deep, just a few feet inside the service line, Ashe decides to hit a delicate dink approach shot at his adversary's feet to try to force him to volley up weakly. This might then allow Ashe to move in and volley the return away for the point.

Figure 22.

Ashe's Dink Shot

Frame a. Ashe here, having run to get in perfect position, exhibits the classic backhand backswing with left hand on the racket, full shoulder turn, elbow bent near the body, racket head high, knees bent and weight a little on the back foot. From this stroke position the opponent is kept guessing whether Ashe will drive, lob or dink. Since the opponent remained deep, Ashe decided to continue with the dink.

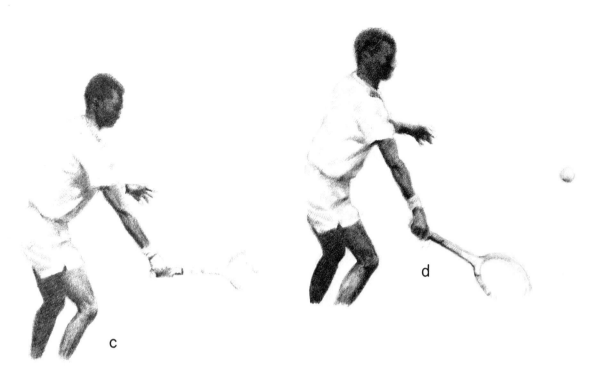

c

d

Frame b. Here Ashe has brought the racket straight down with extended arm and face open to impart sidespin and underspin. His weight, balanced nicely by his left arm, is shifting forward so that he can move quickly toward the net.

Frame c. This frame shows clearly the progress of the stroke as the racket head continues downward after impact with the ball with the face still open and the wrist essentially in line with the racket to direct the ball down the line. The weight is now all on the right foot, knees bent, as Ashe readies his run for the net behind his approach shot.

Frame d. The downward motion of the racket is continued by breaking the wrist. The ball has already reacted to the soft sidespin and underspin stroke and is rising to clear the net and drop gently at the feet of the opposing volleyer. Note that his balance is such that Ashe is starting to move to the net to cut off a hoped-for weak return hit from below the top of the net.

The speed and spin imparted to the ball should be sufficient to make the ball go toward the base line rather than bounce straight up, since a high bounce would allow the receiver to take a step back and make an offensive return.

The Lob

There are two kinds of lobs, offensive and defensive.

The offensive lob is an attempt to win the point by hitting the ball just out of reach over the net player's head, while landing it deep enough in the court with a bounce toward the base line so that the ball cannot be retrieved. It is utilized most when the net player is too close to the net or off balance and the stroker is inside the base line. To be effective, the stroker must hide his intentions until the last moment. Some players hit devastating top-spin lobs which rise and drop sharply and bound drastically toward the backstop for winners. These are too delicate for most players to master as a standard lob. But they are fun to try from time to time. They are usually hit with an eastern or western forehand grip, although Rod Laver can, with his strong wrist, top-spin lob with the continental grip.

The defensive lob is hit high in the air and deep in order to gain time to extricate oneself from an embarrassing defensive situation, usually from behind the base line on the dead run or from a position wide of court.

The method of stroke production is the same as for the standard forehand or backhand drive in its preparation. This provides the hidden intent. The secret of the shot is to keep low, with knees bent, to get under the ball and to follow through high. Figure 23 of Pancho Gonzales, one of the master lobbers, shows him finishing a forehand defensive lob in classic fashion from behind the base line. Except for the top-spin lob, the wrist and elbow should be held reasonably firm. The aim point of the lob is usually to the backhand because few players can hit effectively a backhand from overhead.

A special form of lob used almost exclusively in doubles is the lob volley. It is a beautiful and delicate shot requiring great touch.

Return of Service

In receiving service it is important to take the proper receiving position. To do so first requires a knowledge of the capabilities of the server—how hard he hits the ball and what sort of spin he utilizes. Also the type of court makes a difference, for the bounce is fast on surfaces like grass, cement and asphalt and slower on composition and clay. Figure 24 illustrates the factors to consider in selecting your receiving position.

Figure 23.

Gonzales's Lob

In addition, it is necessary to vary the anticipatory position and moves because of the speed of the ball. Most receivers crouch lower than in the normal anticipatory position and set their feet a bit farther apart. And as the ball is about to be struck by the server, the receiver must study the toss to try to determine whether the serve will be a flat, slice or twist delivery. At the moment of the striking of the ball by the server, most top receivers take a hop up in the air to increase their ability to move rapidly in any direction as dictated by their anticipation and the flight of the ball. A typical receiving anticipatory position and hopping sequence is shown in Figure 25a, page 94. The return of service is one of the most difficult shots to play well, so the good players seem to concentrate more on getting ready for the serve than for any other shot.

Figure 24.

Selecting a Receiving Position

Referring to the backhand court:

One objective of the receiver is to cover the court. In order to be able to reach serves hit to his right or left, he must be near the center of the area to which it is possible to direct serves. As a first step in determining proper position the receiver should note the point from which the server will make his delivery. He should then imagine a point M in the center of the service court, and take his position near the base line on a straight line drawn from the server through point M. For example, if the server stands at A_2, the receiver should stand near F_2, and if the server is at A_3, the receiver should move over to F_3. Some players stand a little to the right or left of the center line if they find their reach or stroke production is better from one side or the other.

Referring to the forehand court:

The straight, flat serve can be delivered only in the area defined by B_2 and B_3. Therefore, the proper receiving position is, as just described, at the midpoint F_1. But this receiving position must be altered if the server imparts spin to the ball. A good slice serve curves to the right and can draw the receiver as much as 10 feet off the court to point B_4, and a twist serve can pull him to left a few feet to point B_1. Therefore, depending on the type of serve he faces, the receiver may be forced to modify his starting position to the right or left of the middle line A_1-M-F_1. In other words, you have to take a position midway between the limits of the *serving area capability* of the particular server opposing you. Thus, you might have to move your initial position from F_1 to midway point C and be prepared to move to the right or left as you note from the server's toss the type of serve he is planning to deliver. This is why knowledge by the receiver of the server's capabilities and anticipation of the server's intentions is so important.

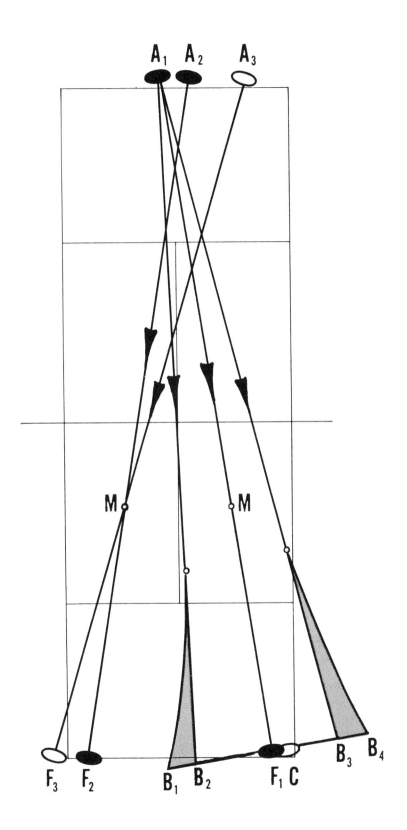

Figure 25.

Backhand Down the Line by Mrs. King

Frame a. Mrs. King is about to receive in the forehand court a serve to her backhand.

Most top players hop slightly as the server is about to strike the ball, since this allows you to be more alert and ready to move quickly to your right or left to intercept serves coming at you at rates up to over 100 miles per hour. Here Mrs. King is slightly off the ground as she makes her preparatory hop just inside the base line.

Frame b. As she comes down she puts her weight on her right foot and starts to pivot to the left and take her racket back.

94

Frame c. Here her backswing is well back, with shoulders turned in proper fashion, as she prepares to meet the ball. A fault of many receivers is that they do not react rapidly enough to execute a full backswing and shoulder turn; so they end up facing the net and pushing rather than stroking the ball.

Frame d. Mrs. King meets the ball well in front of her right foot as she directs it down the line.

Frame e. The follow-through with open racket face indicates an underspin backhand shot. Note that she is working so hard to watch the speeding service ball that she is still looking at the spot of impact.

d

e

Figure 26.

Forehand Down the Line by Mrs. King

Frame a. Mrs. King is about to receive a serve directed at the forehand corner of her forehand court. She has just moved forward, about to make her preparatory hop.

Frame b. Mrs. King has just landed from her hop, turned her left foot slightly and started to push off to her right to meet the ball. Notice that the knees are well flexed and she is all concentration.

Frame c. Her left foot comes over as she starts her racket back with her left hand on it to help force her shoulder turn.

c

b

a

96

Frame d. Here she takes a big stride into the alley to meet the speeding ball. Again she has reacted fast enough to get her backswing completed with proper shoulder and hip turn.

Frame e. Mrs. King brings her left foot forward in a closed stance as she strokes the ball smartly down the line while rotating her shoulders and getting her weight forward. Her eyes are still concentrating on the spot of the impact.

The down-the-line shot from this position is usually preferred, since the server in taking the net cannot get her racket enough to the left of the ball to direct it sharply cross court for a winner. A return cross court, unless a winner, does give up the open side of the court to the volleyer for a placement.

97

Figure 27.

Gonzales's Chip Return of Service

Gonzales's Chip Return of Service

On slow courts the men use the same stroke techniques demonstrated by Mrs. King. But against overpowering serves on fast courts, the men seldom have time to get the racket back as far as the sequences of Mrs. King indicate.

Most players stand no deeper than the base line and try to take the ball on the rise to generate pace on fast returns. For this shot the backswing and follow-through are kept at a level height. Against a net-rushing server it is often better to chip or dink to force the server to volley up from near the net. The chip is hit like a volley with almost no backswing. The dink is hit by sliding the racket around and under the ball as demonstrated by Ashe in the ground stroke in Figure 22, pages 88–89. The master chipper on return of service is Gonzales. Figure 27 shows him just inside the base line at the top of his backswing. Note that he has only had time to turn his shoulders and hips part way, so he is essentially still facing the net-rushing server. By his racket position you can tell he is about to hit a soft, tantalizing, cross court shot just over the net to force the volleyer to hit up a weak backhand return.

CHAPTER 5

Net Play

The ability to play net is absolutely essential to sound tactical tennis, whether singles or doubles. The net is the attacking position from which outright winners are most often hit. In singles on fast courts about 35 percent of winners are hit from the net; on slow courts, 25 to 30 percent. In doubles the speed of the court makes less difference, and some 55 percent of all winners are made from the net position. If you exclude the service and return of service, which must be played from the back court, a staggering 80 percent of all points and 80 percent of all placements in doubles are won at the net position.

Therefore, it is obvious that the budding tennis player must learn how to play net. Fortunately, the volley, overhead and ground strokes at net are fun to hit, and it should be easy to get the novice to practice these strokes. Just being in the commanding attack area is a thrill!

Mrs. King's Standard Forehand Volley

Billie Jean King won a large share of her many amateur and professional singles and doubles titles because of her marvelous net play. In Figure 28 we show her classic style in hitting a low forehand volley.

Ralston's High Backhand Volley—with Something Taken Off

Figure 29 is a sequence of shots showing Dennis Ralston returning a hard forehand drive hit high to his backhand with a volley that

100

Figure 28.

Mrs. King's Standard Forehand Volley

a

b

Frame a. Mrs. King is shown here in the classic anticipatory or ready position with knees bent, weight forward on the balls of the feet, racket in front with head high, cradled in the left hand, and set to volley from either side. Note the great similarity to the ready volleying position of Ralston, shown in Figure 29a, page 104.

Frame b. Here she has pushed off on her left foot and started her shoulder and body turn as she watches and moves toward the approaching ball. Note the short preparation for the backswing with racket high.

101

c

d

Frame c. The reach for the ball is now at the point where the short backswing for the volley is complete, with racket head above the wrist, the knees are bending to get down to the ball, and the left hand is extended for balance.

Frame d. This is the moment of truth as the racket meets the ball 6 to 10 inches in front of the body in perfect form to hit the ball down the line. (A cross court volley would be hit a bit farther forward.) The knees are bent so that the racket head is above the wrist to give a firm hold on the racket (see page 36) and to allow the eyes to follow the ball right onto the strings. The firm wrist is laid back to direct the ball down the line. The racket head is tilted back to create the concave wall, which we described in Figure 7, page 37, and to propel the ball up and over the net at the proper angle. The alert opponent should already be moving to his left to cover the return.

Frame e. Note here that the stiff, laid-back wrist has followed through a short distance while the arm is extended forward only about 8 inches to complete the punching motion guiding the ball crisply, deep down the line. The right knee is so low it almost touches the ground.

Frame f. Finally, Billie Jean has brought her racket forward in perfect balance and is rapidly regaining her ready position to await the opponent's return. Remember that no stroke is completed until you are back in position for the next shot.

e

f

Figure 29.

Ralston's Backhand Volley—
with Something Taken Off

Frame a. Ralston is shown here in a near-classic ready position with weight balanced and knees slightly bent just as he is beginning to move the racket toward his backhand.

Frame b. Note how short the backswing is here at its completion. There are two reasons for this: first, there is not time to permit a longer one as the ball is speeding at Ralston and second, this is all the backswing a good punch (as distinguished from a swinging) volley really needs, for pace is obtained in large part from the speed of the opponent's drive. The left hand is still on the racket, which not only guides it but also helps to make the shoulders turn. The body turn is not quite complete.

c

d

Frame c. This is a beautiful example of form as the racket meets the ball about a foot in front of the body, racket head above the hand to achieve a firm grip with straight, locked wrist. You can just feel the concentration here as Ralston has his eye glued on the ball. Note that the body is now turned perpendicular to the net and the weight is shifting to the forward foot.

Frame d. Just after impact Ralston drops the racket head and simultaneously lays it back at an angle instead of following straight through. This process takes some of the speed out of the volley and keeps the ball inside the base line. The left hand helps to provide balance.

105

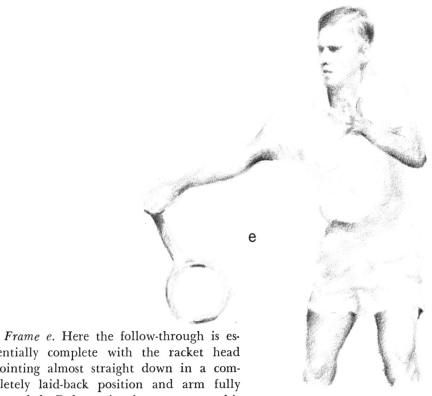

Frame e. Here the follow-through is essentially complete with the racket head pointing almost straight down in a completely laid-back position and arm fully extended. Ralston is about to start his move back to the ready position.

he had to slow down a bit to keep the ball from sailing over the base line. The technique for taking something off the volley is rarely shown in pictures, so this is a particularly interesting sequence.

Figure 29d can be used to explain one other volleying motion for which we do not have a stroking sequence. One of the most difficult volleys to make is one in which the ball is hit right at your stomach. You have to use a backhand volley because the forehand would be too cramped. The way to execute the shot is to move your arm to the right, elbow up, while breaking your wrist and dropping the racket head straight down. Although we recognize that Ralston is not doing just this in Figure 29d, the reader can visualize the small changes needed (elbow higher and bent and racket head straight down and closer to the body) to illustrate the stroke.

Mrs. King's Stop Volley

To best illustrate the differences in racket action in making the

Figure 30.

Mrs. King's Stop Volley

Frame a. To orient the reader, Mrs. King ran her opponent off the court with a drive deep to the forehand corner and took the net. Her opponent answered by a topped cross court forehand drive which dipped low over the net. Since this left the court wide open near the net on the backhand side, Mrs. King decided to dump a little stop volley just over the net near the backhand sideline.

As the ball approaches, Billie Jean is bending her waist and knees to get her line of vision near the trajectory of the ball and her racket head along the line of her wrist. Her left hand is extended for balance.

Frame b. This figure shows the very short backswing prior to hitting the stop volley. As in all good volleys the wrist leads the racket and the ball will be struck in front of the body so that its flight can be followed all the way into the racket. Her eyes are concentrating on the ball. She is about to slide the racket under the ball, the first clue to the stop volley.

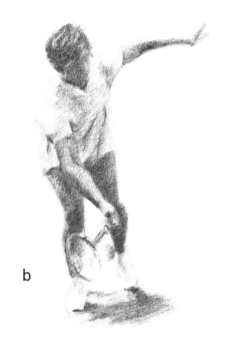

b

a

107

c

Frame c. Here we see the real secret of the stop volley. Instead of following through with a firm punching action as in Figure 28e, page 103, Mrs. King is letting her racket rebound backward from the force of impact of the ball. This entails a breaking wrist action and an open racket face to give lift to the flight of the ball. The extent of the negative follow-through is clearly shown as it causes the ball to float slowly upward, clearing the net with room to spare and plopping dead in the opponent's forecourt for an easy placement.

A delicate shot such as this is not recommended for the beginner, since it obviously requires perfect touch, and sometimes an element of surprise, in order to bring off a winner.

stop volley from the action in the standard volley, we have elected to show the same player, Mrs. Billie Jean King, hitting the volley (Figure 30). You can easily contrast this shot with the crisp, deep volley shown in Figure 28d, page 102.

The Swinging Volley

The standard, short punch volley just demonstrated by Mrs. King can be changed to a much more offensive swinging volley if the ball is traveling not too fast and is a foot or two above net level so that you can hit down or at an angle without fear of hitting the ball out. See Figure 31.

The Overhead

The overhead is one of the most difficult strokes to hit well consistently, as the ball not only drops down toward you at varying angles, but wind and sun often combine to add to your positioning and timing problems. It is absolutely essential, therefore, to get ready for the shot as early as possible and to watch the ball with great care. In Figure 32 we see Mrs. King executing the shot with grace and perfection.

Figure 31.

Ashe's Swinging Volley

a

Frame a. Ashe is starting to move rapidly to his right to volley a return which he sees will be high enough to present a perfect opportunity for a hard, swinging volley placement. His backswing is starting as he pushes off with his left foot, knees bent and balance perfect.

b

c

Frame b. Ashe now has completed his backswing as his racket points straight back toward the base line. Contrast this with the short backswing by Mrs. King in Figure 28c, page 102.

Frame c. Ashe has now given away his intent, since he is reaching beyond the ball so that he can hit a sharp cross court volley. His left foot is about to cross the right as it also moves forward, which is another signal that he will hit the ball ahead of his body in the cross court direction. The smart receiver should be ready at this second to move to his right to try to retrieve the volley.

Frame d. Here Ashe is about to stroke the volley well in front of his body at an acute cross court angle. His knees are bent as his body moves forward, some momentum still carrying him to the right. His eyes are concentrating on the ball.

Frame e. At the completion of the swinging volley, Ashe has followed through, with racket face slightly open, so that the racket is starting up toward his left shoulder just as in the finish of a forehand ground stroke. His knees are well bent, and his left hand has moved to the right to balance the momentum of his swing. Contrast the long follow-through with the punching motion, wrist leading, used by Mrs. King in Figure 28e, page 103.

This volley resulted in a screaming placement.

111

Figure 32.

Mrs. King's Overhead

Frame a. Here we catch Mrs. King at the end of the preparatory hop as she *turns* and pushes off with her left foot to move back to get under the lob.

Frame b. As she starts to move back she immediately raises her racket, which is a necessary motion to get ready for the stroke.

Frame c. Note that as she turns and continues rapidly backward she watches the ball very intently. The problems of wind and sun make it absolutely essential to watch the ball right into the racket.

d

e

f

Frame d. At the start of the backswing she has her racket arm straight, knees bent, body sideways to the net, left arm out for balance and eyes on the approaching ball.

Frame e. She is now in turned position under the ball as she continues her backswing, racket high and left arm extended. She is setting her weight on her right foot with knees bent ready to leap.

Frame f. Now the backswing is complete, the racket head pointing straight down as in the service stroke. She has leaped about a foot off the court with her right foot while the left hand comes down to maintain perfect balance. The leap allows her to hit down on the ball, giving a greater court target zone.

113

Frame g. At the moment of impact the racket arm is straight as in the serve, the right foot comes forward to put her weight into the shot while the left hand is tucked in and the body turns in the direction of the shot. From her position you can see she is aiming the smash at her opponent's backhand corner. The ball is hit almost flat, as this not only is easier to do, but spin takes speed off of the shot. Her body is tilted back slightly to propel the ball deep in the court. The opponent better be on her bicycle by now to have a chance of returning this one.

Frame h. Mrs. King has completed the scissor movement of the legs now as her right foot comes forward and her left foot comes down on the court. Note the beautiful wrist action as she brings the racket head down with great force in her follow-through. The footwork, balance and grace are such that a dancer would be proud of this sequence of actions!

Frame i. The stroke is now completed with a long follow-through, and Mrs. King is already turning to move rapidly back to the net and the ready position.

114

CHAPTER 6

Improving Your Game

Once you have learned the basic individual strokes, the next problem is how to put them all together to mold them into a sound game. It takes much more than proper stroke execution to win at tennis. Although there are several acceptable ways of producing each stroke, there are limitless ways to utilize them, because of the many combinations of player physiques, capabilities, types and speed of strokes, court positions of the participants, court surfaces, weather conditions and so on. True courtcraft involves sound execution, tactics, anticipation, physical fitness and psychology. This includes the ability to analyze your opponent's game—strokes, footwork, habits, likes and dislikes—in order to formulate a proper game plan, and develop the resourcefulness to seize opportunities. The complexities of tennis are what make it such a fabulous game. We have tried to show you simple, neat and tidy stroke production methods so that you can build from this sound foundation to the extent of your own particular capabilities.

In effect, what you must do is array your game against the opponent. If he likes to volley, try to keep him away from the net. If he thrives on pace, feed him soft floaters and spin. If he hates net play, bring him in to the forecourt. Since the backhand is usually the weaker side, the forehand down the line and backhand cross court are standard offensive shots. But you cannot play his weakness too often, lest it turn into a strength.

One of the major reasons a tennis player must have a basic understanding of tactics is that there is so little time during the course of producing a stroke in which to think about the best shot to make. Thus through understanding and knowledge developed by coaching, study and practice, the accomplished player must create the ability to produce the best shot almost automatically. Often he is not

115

aware of really thinking about the shot as he takes in the tactical situation in a glance and essentially makes the proper play instinctively. But do not be misled. Behind this seemingly natural capability there exists a storehouse of tactical knowledge which the great player is able to tap instantaneously. Only in exceptional cases does a player arrive on the tennis scene who can win by the sheer power of his strokes. Even so, his opponents usually find ways of blunting his weapons so that his reign is indeed short-lived, unless he too resorts to brainy tactics.

Only a summary of important basic tactics can be presented in this chapter. Therefore the reader who is anxious to delve deeper into this vital aspect of the game is advised to read also the authors' previously published books on the tactics of singles and doubles.[1]

Tactics for singles play differ substantially from those required for doubles. Therefore, we will briefly discuss the two separately.

Singles Tactics

If on the mind of the student of singles tactics there could be indelibly printed only two words, we would select steadiness and depth. Ability to keep the ball in play is the hallmark of all great singles players, and the backbone of the successful attacking game is maintaining depth of the service, ground and volley strokes.

As tennis matches are normally scored, errors (approximately equally split between nets and outs) account for about 60 percent of points won, and placements, including service aces, account for 40 percent. These percentages reveal clearly the overwhelming importance of steadiness, or getting the ball back. However, perhaps the true advantage of the attacking game can be more realistically illustrated by two other examples. First, if one is allowed to add to the placements those points where the stroker is judged to have played the ball so effectively as to force an error on the part of the receiver, then the attacking game wins about 60 percent of the points by placements, and errors account for only the remaining 40 percent. And second, strokes made from the attacking position at net, which is gained only after employing forcing tactics, are the most lethal

1 *The Game of Singles in Tennis* (Philadelphia: J. B. Lippincott Company, 1962). *The Game of Doubles in Tennis* (Philadelphia: J. B. Lippincott Company, 1956).

in tennis and thus provide a major share (about one third) of outright winners.

In modern offensive tennis the most important stroke is the service because it is responsible for approximately 40 percent of all winners through aces, errors or weak returns which can then be put away by later volleys or forcing ground strokes. On slower surfaces, such as clay courts, the big serve is not nearly so important. The fraction of a second more time the slower bounce takes allows the receiver, believe it or not, to be twice as effective. You should concentrate on getting the first serve in as much as 70 percent of the time and on hitting every serve deep. The experts do both about 80 percent of the time. Just getting the serve deep should permit you to win roughly 74 percent of your service points, since it gives you the advantage of starting most points on the offensive. Equipped with a good toss and the proper service grip, you should also be able to mix up the speed, spin and placement of the serve so that the receiver cannot assume a stereotyped delivery and is thus kept off balance.

In general, on a fast court the big-serve exponents aim first serves deep to the outside corner to run the receiver wide and open up the court for an easy first-volley placement. Second serves are usually hit deep to the backhand corner in both courts. This is the best tactic for most players, with emphasis on keeping the ball deep (within 3 feet of the service line).

The return of service is probably the most difficult stroke in tennis to hit consistently. But hit it consistently you must if you are going to stand a chance of breaking your opponent's serve and winning the match. Just getting the ball back turns the odds of winning the point from 2 or 3 to 1 against you to even! First, you have to learn how to position yourself for receiving the serve. Even though there are a number of factors to consider, depending on the ability of the server, it is generally best to stand 1 to 3 feet inside the base line on a straight line drawn from the position of the server through a point in the center of the service court. On a second serve it is ordinarily best to move in another 1 to 3 feet. These receiving positions shorten the distance you have to move to one side or the other for a breaking serve and allow you to hit the ball sooner and on the rise in order to hurry the server. Against a top server, you must also try to anticipate from his toss and actions what type of serve he will hit in order to get a start in the right direction to reach a 100-mile-an-hour bullet.

The best aim points for the receiver depend on whether the server is rushing the net or remaining on the base line. These points are shown in the two diagrams in Figure 33, and should be firmly imprinted upon the mind of the aspiring singles player.

Figure 33.

Aim Points for Return of Service

Against the net-rushing server the object is to hit the ball by him or to force him to reach for the volley to blunt its effectiveness or to make him hit up from his shoe tops a weak volley or half volley. The thing to avoid at all costs is hitting into the danger area, which will hand the server gift points two out of three times. Down-the-line shots are best made from serves hit to the outside, although short down-the-line shots can be made from serves near the middle. Returns to the center must be made early from well inside the base line in order to hit the server at his feet while he is still moving in the vicinity of the service line. Obviously, the short serve is the answer to the prayer of every receiver, since he can bang it to any one of the preferred aim points. And the ability to mix up his returns in order to keep the server guessing adds tasty frosting to the cake.

Against the server who stays back at the base line the object is to hit the return deep, that is, to within 10 feet of the base line. Down-the-line or cross court shots to areas A and C have the advantage of forcing the server to run. On a short serve it is often possible to win the point outright by a sharp cross court drive to areas D and E or, occasionally, by faking a drive and playing a soft drop shot. The latter is particularly effective in ladies' play. Once again, returns of service to the danger area will lose two out of three points.

118

Server

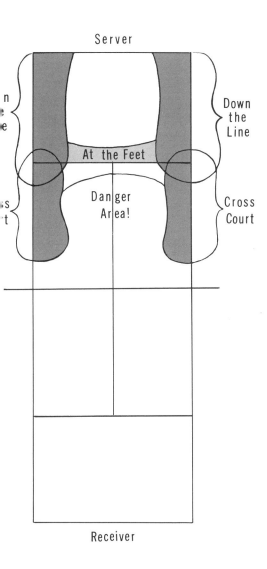

n
e

s
t

Down
the
Line

At the Feet

Danger
Area!

Cross
Court

Receiver

Server

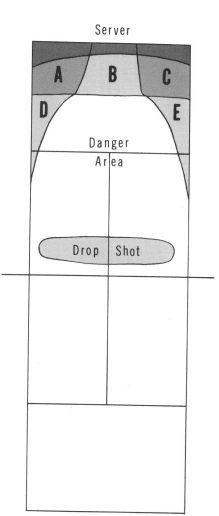

A   B   C

D   E

Danger
Area

Drop   Shot

Receiver

Tennis is a percentage game, and the percentages favor the attacker. Therefore every effort of the player during the progress of the point should be directed toward obtaining the best attacking position, which is at the net. In topflight tennis, from one fourth to one third of all points are won at net. Volleys and overheads are the most lethal shots in tennis because they give the opponent so little time to defend his court that they produce outright winners a high percentage of the time.

Actually, the net position is the dominant court position only when you have made the proper preparation for your advance through a forcing approach shot. Without this, even the best volleyer will be vulnerable to the passing shots of any competent opponent. To help you keep this point in mind, always remember that the good volley is really an approach shot and volley combination. Ordinarily, most forcing approach shots, whether serves, returns of service, volleys, ground strokes or offensive lobs, must be hit deep.

If you and your opponent are exchanging shots from the base line, the best tactic by far is to keep the ball deep. In fact, the whole base line game is one of fencing with the opponent until you can force him to hit a shallow return. Once such an opening occurs, it is imperative that you capitalize on it by moving in and hitting for an outright winner or by playing a forcing shot and moving in to the net for the kill. Since seven out of eight base line duels are won by one player moving in to net to take advantage of a short return, it is absolutely essential that you waste no opportunities to take the offensive. Otherwise all your artistic base line fencing will have been for naught. By a shallow return, we mean one bouncing more than 10 feet inside your base line. You really need this kind of advantage for two major reasons. First, you should be able to play a more offensive forcing shot, deep or angled, the closer you are to the net. And second, and even more important, you need the time to complete your run in to the preferred volleying position (6 to 9 feet from the net). If you start your ground stroke from too far back in your court, your opponent may well be able to grab the offensive by hitting his return early at your feet as you advance in the vicinity of the service line, where you are most liable to err or to volley ineffectively.

To recapitulate, the objective of the approach or forcing shot is to make the defender hit a weak return and to allow you time to get into the best volleying position. Ideally your approach shot

120

should run the defender deep and wide to either side to open up the entire cross court area for an easy volley placement. Against most players, a drive deep to the backhand is most likely to draw the weakest return. And, given a choice, it is better to hit the approach shot down the line, as this provides the striker with a short trip to the proper volleying position. This position is a foot or two on the down-the-line side of center, since the opponent can hit a faster down-the-line passing shot simply because such a drive cross court would sail over the sideline.

Once a duel begins between a net player and a passer on the base line, the importance of depth becomes paramount. As long as the passer is kept pinned back by balls bouncing within 10 feet of the base line, the volleyer should win about eight out of ten exchanges because he has time to intercept the returns with the option of angling for a winner or hitting deep to keep the passer on the defensive. However, if the ball lands between the service line and a point 10 feet inside the base line, the odds shift in favor of the passer, and he should be able to win about two out of three exchanges. And if the ball bounces on or inside the service line and the passer is alert and able to reach the ball, he should pass the volleyer a resounding seven out of eight times. Thus, the overwhelming importance of depth to the approach shot and volley player is obvious and must be remembered at all times. On the other hand, the passer must be alert to take advantage of any gifts sent his way in the form of a short volley.

Next, let us impress upon you the need for steadiness, or keeping the ball in play, by recounting the horrors of errors:

25 percent of all service returns are errors. But if you can just return the ball, your chances of winning the point become even.

25 percent of all first volleys are errors. But if you can make the volley, only half will be returned and the odds turn in the server's favor.

And if the receiver can return the serve and the first volley, he will have a better than even chance of winning the point.

Overall, about 50 percent of all points lost in tennis are caused by errors.

This explains why the steady players, like Rosewall and Laver, and the great retrievers, like Grant and Gonzales, are so hard to beat at singles. Those retrievers, when seemingly hopelessly out of the point, always manage to play a shot that gives them time to get back into position and turn apparently lost points into winners. Never give up the ship!

Finally, to become a great player you must not only practice diligently to overcome weaknesses, but participate in tournaments to sharpen your competitive edge and will to win. More about this later.

Doubles Tactics

The first basic step toward playing good doubles is to form a team, and this encompasses much more than just having two players on the same side of the net. It takes at least two or three years of practicing, playing, planning and working together to form a team coordinated on offense and defense. This is because of the many factors involved, such as knowing the type of shot or tactical move your partner will probably employ under a multitude of circumstances so you can optimally position yourself for the return, knowing who should take shots down the middle, diagnosing together answers for the strategy of the opposition, developing means for exploiting the weaknesses of the opponents, encouraging one another in overcoming the sad trials of mental or stroke lapses. Teamwork alone accounts for about 25 percent of the success of a doubles combine.

A second basic step is to develop the fine art of anticipation. As noted in detail later in this chapter, the only way to be ready for the return and in the correct position at the proper split second is to diagnose what the striking opponent will do, based upon the position of his racket arm, backswing and feet, and his habits and favorite shots. This is particularly true in doubles because of the many rapid volley exchanges at point-blank range. And it is important to remember that the opponents are also endeavoring to anticipate, so that you must both vary and hide your shots in order to gain the advantage of deception.

The serve is considered the single most important shot in doubles because it wins about 20 percent of all points outright and also places the serving team in the offensive position as the server moves in to net to volley successful returns. The aim of the server should be to get the first serve in deep about 80 percent of the time, for he has almost twice as good a chance to win with the first as compared to the second serve (because the receiver moves in to a more offensive position on the weaker second serve). To get the first serve in and consistently deep, and to gain time to run in to the net position, most servers resort to the American twist hit to the backhand corner at about three-fourths speed. The flat and slice serves are used to keep the receiver honest.

The partner of the server at net should note the type and bounce point of the serve, study the receiver to anticipate his return and be prepared to move to establish the best offensive formation, to poach or to cover a lob. Some top net players often signal their poaches to keep the opponents psychologically off balance as well as to inform the server so he can cover the vacated side.

The return of service is the most difficult shot in doubles, since it must be played with great precision if it is to cause the serving team trouble. The most effective shot is a low, dipping cross court dink or top-spin drive that forces the server to volley up and permits the receiving team to move in to the net position to volley offensively. If the receiver can carry out this assignment, there is a tremendous payoff because he turns the odds of winning the point from 2 to 1 against him to 2 to 1 in his favor. To keep the opponents guessing, the receiver must lob occasionally and drive down the line against a poaching net man. But by all odds the most important thing is to get the ball back, as there is always the chance of a serving team error even on the feeblest of returns. The partner of the receiver at the modified net position (near the T) should note quickly the type and direction of the return of service, glimpse any move by the opposing net man to poach and watch the type of first volley the server is about to play. So alerted, the modified net man can often make impossible gets or drift to the center to put away weak first volleys by the server.

Net play is what wins most doubles matches. Excluding service or return of service winners, which must be played from the backcourt, an overwhelming 80 percent of all winners and 80 percent of all placements are made at the net.

Net play starts with the first volley, 85 percent of which are made by the server as he moves in to the net position. If the return is weak or high, the server or poaching net man should be able to win the point immediately. If, however, the return of service is so expert as to force the server to volley up, the receiving team should be able to move in and volley back a winner.

In about half the cases, the point is not won on the ordinarily difficult-to-stroke first volley made by the server, and a battle ensues. Generally such first volleys should be hit deep near the center by the server or at the feet of an advancing receiver. The maneuvering strategy on a volley exchange is to hit first to the center to open up the alleys for an angled winner or to angle first to open up the center for the deep, crisp winner. In the absence of an opening, a shot between the two opponents often draws an error. In many cases soft volleys at the feet of the opponents cause the ball to be hit up for an explosive, winning answer. Soft volleys also prevent the opponent from obtaining pace on his return. In any event, touch is vital, for overhitting the setups, such as shallow lobs, leads to errors, and underhitting allows the opponents to turn "lost" points into gets and eventual winners.

While base line play is to be avoided in doubles because only 20 percent of points are won from the backcourt, do not give up just because you are out of position. It is vital to learn how to hit low, dipping drives or dinks that will permit you to move in on a weak return volley, and to play offensive passing shots for winners or lobs that will drive the opponents away from the net. Avoid at all costs hitting a shot that allows the opponents to catch your partner out of position. For example, if he is at net, do not hit down the line to give the opposing net man an easy cross court volley winner into the open diagonal area.

In brief, you must learn courtcraft, by which we mean selecting and playing the proper shot so that you and your partner can work in unison to best position yourselves for the expected return in order to be able to force the opening you need for the winner. Calling shots "in" or "out" and calling "yours" and "mine" on shots either might play are key points in achieving true team play. It is particularly helpful to call serves to your partner's court, since you are in a perfect position to do so at the modified net position, and it allows your partner to concentrate entirely on watching and playing the ball. Once you learn the fundamentals of the game, you can reap great pleasure from sharpening your anticipation, your ability to maneuver for the all-important opening, your consistency and your molding of team play. Doubles is, most assuredly, among the greatest of all team sports.

124

Anticipation Explained

Repeatedly in many paragraphs of this and preceding chapters we have referred to the importance of anticipation. Although anticipation is also mentioned as vital in writings on other sports, it turns out to be a most difficult art to explain, even to an eager student. The great players develop an instinct, or sixth sense, to predict the opponent's return and move at the proper moment to intercept the ball. This they accomplish by a four-step process:

1. From the placement and type of his own shot, the anticipator begins by having some idea what sort of reply to expect and can start to position himself for the return.

2. Through study of his opponent, the anticipator has knowledge of the stroking style, habits, favorite shots in various tactical situations and giveaway motions of the opponent's shot-making techniques.

3. Based on the knowledge from step 2, the anticipator should now concentrate not on the ball but on the motions of the opponent as he is about to stroke the ball. By noting the position of his feet, body, arm, length and direction of backswing and position of the racket with respect to the ball, he can diagnose the type and direction of the return. (Whereas this may sound complicated, practice will allow you to do this at a glance.)

4. The final step requires that the anticipator time his move to intercept the return to the proper split second. Moving too soon will allow the opponent to alter his return, and moving too late will mean failure to get to the ball.

We decided the only way to clarify this complex subject for the reader would be to take some high-speed movies of an actual anticipation sequence and to analyze the movements. As far as we are aware, this has never been done before, since it entails employing a special camera angle from within the area of the court surface in order to get both players in view simultaneously. Fortunately, we were able to catch Billie Jean King and Kathy Harter in a practice session, and they kindly obliged us with a number of exchanges until we obtained within movie camera angle an excellent example of successful anticipation. Selected frames depicting proper stroke production techniques are shown in Figure 34, pages 126–30.

125

Figure 34.

Anticipation Sequence by Mrs. King

The reader should direct special attention to this fascinating sequence of Kathy Harter (in warm-up togs) and Mrs. King as they demonstrate anticipation. Mrs. King is at net, and Miss Harter is hitting from near the service line, from which position she should easily pass Billie Jean down the line or cross court about three or four out of five times.

a

Frame a. Mrs. King is at net in the ready position while the ball starts to rise toward Miss Harter as she takes her racket back in classic fashion, with weight on her left foot and her left hand on the racket. At this time Kathy is uncommitted and can hit the ball either down the line or cross court.

126

b

Frame b. As the ball continues to rise, Kathy shifts her weight as she watches the ball and also takes a peek at Billie Jean's position. As of this moment neither player is committed to hit or to move in either direction, and the duel of deception is at its peak.

Kathy could reach far left and hit over the ball cross court, hit straight at Billie Jean or hit down the line to her left.

c

d

Frame c. At this split second it now becomes apparent that Kathy will hit down the line for three reasons. First, the ball is getting past the point where she can reach out and hit it early enough to go cross court. Second, her wrist is beginning to lead the racket in a down-the-line direction. And third, Kathy has planted her right foot and body in perfect closed-stance position for a shot down the sideline. Billie Jean, having noted in a flash, through experience, all these telltale signs, has pushed off with her left foot and started toward her right. This is the key moment of her anticipatory process.

f

e

Frame d. At the second Kathy strikes the ball with racket hand leading her racket, Billie Jean has moved her weight toward her right foot and moved her racket to her forehand side.

Frame e. As the ball moves over the net it is apparent that Billie Jean has started her shoulder turn for the volley and pushed off harder with her left foot.

Frame f. Here the ball is still well to Billie Jean's right as she strides far toward the sideline with racket back and shoulders fully turned.

g

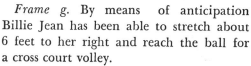

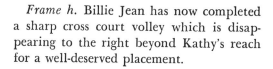

Frame g. By means of anticipation Billie Jean has been able to stretch about 6 feet to her right and reach the ball for a cross court volley.

Frame h. Billie Jean has now completed a sharp cross court volley which is disappearing to the right beyond Kathy's reach for a well-deserved placement.

h

Without the 6-foot anticipatory effort on the part of Billie Jean, this point would have resulted in any easy passing shot winner for Kathy. In more complex sequences the striker or the volleyer may fake a shot or a move in order to cause the opponent to make the wrong decision. Success in thus confusing the adversary and converting a seemingly lost cause into a winning point usually forces even the most serious player to break out in an inward grin of self-satisfaction.

To emphasize further the tremendous importance of anticipation, we decided to monitor the finals of United States professional singles championship between Rod Laver and another top professional. In order to record anticipation, we had to invent a new method of watching a tennis match. The reason for this is that you have to be wall-eyed in the extreme to be able to watch both stroker and receiver at the same instant. This is really a sad fact, as it causes spectators to miss one of the most exciting features of a tennis match—the instantaneous duel between the stroker trying to hide his intentions and the receiver trying to anticipate the return. Such a duel is most clearly staged when one player is at net and the stroker is trying to pass or lob him.

To monitor this important match one of the authors enlisted the services of his long-suffering doubles partner, Gilbert M. Roddy. We sat beside each other behind the base line, and Gil watched the passer as the author concentrated on the net player. At the moment the stroker hit the ball, Gil punched the author's leg while noting on paper the position and actions of the stroker. Immediately, the author, watching the movements of the net player, determined whether he had anticipated the passing shot or lob by moving in the proper direction before the impact of Gil's punch, and also recorded the return and outcome of the point. (The people in nearby seats thought we were nuts, but at least the punching routine kept the noise pollution low.) The results were most revealing. In fact, the whole tennis match turned on the duel between the volleying anticipator and the clever passer.

As you might expect, if the passer was in the forecourt inside a point about 6 feet behind the service line, the net player was dead. Either stroker in this advantageous, close position passed or lobbed his opponent successfully eight out of nine times.

However, the story was entirely different in the area of the true duel, which is when the passer is from about 6 feet inside to 2 feet behind the base line. Here Laver's hiding capabilities as a passer and anticipatory power as a volleyer so excelled his opponent that we are withholding his name out of kindness. Laver enjoyed an 8 or 9 to 1 advantage over his opponent in terms of success in passing or in volleying away a winner. By his deceptive wrist action he was able to fool his opponent by hiding the direction and type of passing shot a majority of the time. And Laver, as the volleyer, was able to anticipate the opponent's passing shot and volley it away four out of five times. These superior passing and volleying assets led Laver to an easy, straight-set victory.

The additional intriguing fact that showed in the data we collected was that Laver, in the role of the anticipating volleyer, seldom had to move more than one full step to intercept the return. This was because he had carried out so proficiently steps 1 and 2 of the aforementioned anticipation process that he had properly positioned himself at net for the return. By way of contrast, Laver so well disguised his passing shots and lobs that his opponent was caught flat-footed and never took more than half a step in the right direction as the ball often sailed past him. We would be a bit unfair to Laver's opponent if we failed to mention that left-handers are something else—their spin and directions are unusual, unexpected and downright baffling.

The lesson here is clear. In no other way can we emphasize so positively the importance of being one step in the right direction in a championship tennis match. Even if you are an Olympic sprinter you cannot possibly cover the area of a 27-by-39-foot tennis court, unless you can learn to anticipate successfully. Therefore, we implore our readers to master this fascinating art. The impact of anticipation on tactics is brought out in our books on singles and doubles.

Practicing and Conditioning

The extent to which a player should practice and condition himself depends, of course, on the individual and his particular motivations. The male player aiming for the tournament circuit must work hard if he is to be able to play at peak form on successive days long, five-set matches. The topflight women must also work, although not quite as resolutely as the men. But the weekend player is often limited in his ability to practice, either by lack of time and court availability or by a tendency to develop stiff or sore muscles which prevent him from enjoying his usual friendly game.

For purposes of this section, we will assume you are truly determined to become a competent player. We will present a description of probably the most rigorous type of practicing and conditioning, that utilized by international players. You can then back off from this to suit your own level of ambition.

Instead of using the whole court for practice, the ranking players often use only half the doubles court. This allows you to hit and to retrieve many more shots during the course of a practice session, and to learn to achieve greater accuracy under the pressure of a limited hitting target. The selected practice area can be varied in many ways. You can practice forehand or backhand, base line, base line versus net, or net play, from all angles. Thus you can play down either line by using either half the width of the court, or cross court by using either diagonal half of the court.

The experts practice by trying to hit winners against one another whether they are both on the base line or at net or whether one is at net and the other is trying to pass him, lob him, dink him or put together combinations thereof to beat him from the back court or to take the net away. Usually they have a dozen or more balls at their disposal, so they can keep the rallies going at the rapid pace guaranteed to develop balance and agility, take off excess weight and build endurance. This type of endurance is better than that developed only through conventional roadwork because you have to face the more realistic quick start, change of direction and anticipatory type of running actually required in tennis play. Billie Jean King told the writers that this type of practice, which she first used in Australia in 1966, did more to develop her game than any other thing she could remember.

A half hour of this form of concentrated practice is more than most players can take. Thus you should be able to find out quickly what your own stroke or court coverage weaknesses are. Then you can strive to convert these into strong points and thereby build the confidence so vitally needed in the character of any competent player.

The Australians also have a good method of practicing volley exchanges at the net. They place two on one side hitting volleys against a single net player on the other side and then rotate so everyone gets plenty of experience.

Conditioning goes beyond the practice of playing tennis. Depending on the characteristics of the individual, it includes proper diet, rest and muscle development. Many players squeeze tennis or squash balls to improve finger and grip strength and work with weights and setting up exercises to develop arm, shoulder, leg and stomach tone. Running backward is helpful in acquiring the knack of backpedaling to turn otherwise good lobs into effective overhead returns. And it is necessary to learn to jump high to reach the best lobs. Proper conditioning is necessary to permit you to survive a three-hour match and maintain the necessary concentration at the same time. It obviates tenseness and irritability which reduce effectiveness.

During the progress of a match it is important to know your own limitations with respect to such things as liquids, heat, cold, oxygen and recuperative powers. Most players refrain from drinking quantities of liquids and just rinse a dry mouth or take brief sips. Some require hats, even water-soaked hats, for protection from the sun. At medium altitudes it is helpful to take fairly deep breaths while waiting between points. At high altitudes this extra supply of oxygen is imperative. Certain players have a remarkable capacity to regain composure and strength just when they appear ready to collapse. Part of this ability is sheer courage and determination. Much of this power of recovery is mental discipline. Whenever Bitsy Grant, the Mighty Atom, ran himself into a state of near exhaustion, he used to force himself to walk with short, bouncy steps as though he had just begun to play. This literally placed him back on his toes with a fresh outlook, and soon he was once again ready to fly all over the court. This sort of fighting comeback is, to say the least, rather discouraging to the morale of the opposition.

Older players require a fairly long warm-up to avoid muscle pulls. And they need all the physical conditioning possible in order to be mentally enough alert to keep reminding themselves to bend those tired old knees, turn those weary shoulders and focus those dimming eyes on that little white ball.

Finally, do not forget that an important adjunct of practicing is taking lessons from competent teachers. Even top players can develop bad habits which they find difficult to self-diagnose, but which can often be spotted immediately upon careful scrutiny by a professional or fellow player.

Influence of Court Surface on Play

Tennis is played on a variety of surfaces the world over, such as grass, cement, asphalt, composition and clay. Whereas the variations in surface texture should not significantly affect doubles tactics, the slight differences in speed and height of bounce drastically affect singles play. The fraction of a second longer that the ball stays in the air on a clay court versus the faster grass allows a player to cover a few feet more of court area and thus not only retrieve many more balls but also gain the necessary time to execute more effectively a great number of shots.

We recently overheard at Forest Hills a ranking tennis player from the south summing up the situation succinctly in this way: "Here on the grass you hit the big serve, run to the net, punch that crisp volley and the point is over. Down south on our clay you can hit that big serve, run to the net, punch that crisp volley and, man, the point is just barely beginning!"

The truth lodged in this amusing observation is borne out by the record books. The grass-court champions tend to be the big serve and volley artists like Budge, Kramer, Gonzales and Laver, and the complete players like Rosewall. However, the slower surface clay-court champions tend to be the steady ground stroke and phenomenal retriever greats such as Cochet, Grant, Parker, Riggs and Rosewall. Only Tilden, the master, appears frequently in the lists of champions irrespective of court surface.

To get a quick understanding of a few of the variables in play and equipment brought about by court surface, the reader is advised to study the table on page 136.

Court Manners

A fitting subject upon which to end this book is etiquette on the court. Ethics play a more important part in tennis than in most sports, partly because a player, in the absence of linesmen, is responsible for calling the shots of his opponent. It is imperative that a player establish a reputation for fairness on calls, or he will find his ability to obtain willing opponents jeopardized. An unwritten rule is "When in doubt, call the ball good." In doubles, partners should assist each other on calls. In addition, you should learn the rules of tennis thoroughly so that any misunderstandings on foot faults, replay of points, continuity of play and other important technicalities will be minimized.

True sportsmanship is a vital ingredient in developing your game and maximizing your enjoyment from tennis. This entails not only fair play and control of emotions (even on "bad" calls), but also courtesy. Consideration of others must include your opponent, partner, spectators, hard-working officials, ball boys, players on the next court and people waiting for a court. And do not forget your obligations to encourage questions and help the aspiring youngster at all times. Finally, you men should be willing to play with the charming women from time to time. After all, this is your contribution toward making the little darlings even more beautiful!

In parting, we wish you all good bounces, the best of luck, enjoyment and continued improvement in your tennis play!

Table
Major Tennis Court Differences

	Fast Court Grass	Intermediate Court Cement or Asphalt	Slow Court Synthetic Com- position or Clay
Surface Texture	Fast; speed dependent on length and type of grass and hardness of ground underneath.	Rather fast; speed dependent on grain of the concrete or asphalt.	Slow; speed dependent on type of clay, dry or wet, granular or sticky.
Bounce	Grass stains make ball heavier and slower in flight, but bounce is fast, low and skidding, particularly when spin is imparted.	Wear rapidly smooths the ball, making it fast in flight and bounce.	Clay can stick to or defuzz the ball to affect its time of flight, but the ball bites into the soft surface, and the bounce is reasonably high and slow.
Footwork	Move at ball with fast, short, sure steps. Play the ball rather than let the ball play you.	Same as grass, but steps can be longer, depending on maneuverability.	Plenty of time to run and reach the ball; sometimes sliding into the shot is preferred on a granular surface.
Racket Handling	Uncertainty of bounce dictates shortened backswing and follow-through of racket.	Backswing and follow-through of intermediate length.	Longer strokes and lighter racket are standard.
Anticipation	With fast play you have to concentrate on foreseeing the opponent's intentions, or you cannot succeed.	Here, too, the fast bounce means you have to be a jump ahead of the ball.	Although you can get away with less exact anticipation, you must read your opponent if you wish to be a winner.
Racket Stringing	Thin-gauge gut, tight stringing—58 to 65 lbs. tension.	Thin-gauge gut, fairly tight.	Heavy-gauge gut, looser stringing— 48 to 60 lbs. tension.
Shoes	Grip soles are standard. For wet surface, be prepared with spikes.	Smooth-sole sneakers are best.	Smooth soles are generally good, but grip soles are needed on granular surface.